Dear Ka,
Thank[you for your] wonderful [showing] an interest in my family's history.
Much gratitude,
Lori

4,456 Miles:
A Survivor's Search For Closure

Awakening Her Daughter's Search For Understanding The Holocaust

By Lori Klisman Ellis

4,456 Miles:
A Survivor's Search for Closure

Awakening Her Daughter's Search For Understanding The Holocaust

by Lori Klisman Ellis

Published by

ARKETT PUBLISHING
division of Arkettype
PO Box 36, Gaylordsville, CT 06755
806-350-4007 • Fax 860-355-3970
www.arkett.com

Copyright © 2019 Lori Klisman Ellis

All rights reserved under International and Pan-American Copyright Conventions. No part of this book may be reproduced or transmitted by any means without permission in writing from the author. Illustrations may not be reproduced or transmitted by any means without permission in writing from the illustrator.

ISBN 978-1-69-585631-8

Printed in USA.

Dedication

This book is dedicated to my loving father, Bernard Klisman. May his memory be a blessing to all those that knew him and loved him. He was a hard-working and honest man who dedicated himself to his family. He, along with my mother, never wanted to talk about the Holocaust to their children because he wanted them (Mark and Lori) to be happy and well adjusted. He can be seen in Monni Must's book *Living Witnesses—Faces of the Holocaust*. He can also be seen on *Portraits of Honor* at the Holocaust Memorial Center in Farmington Hills, MI. or online at www.portraitsofhonor.org.

I also dedicate this book to my beautiful mother, Sophie Klisman; a strong, brave and loving woman who lived by the mantra of "hope." She started a new life in the USA and tried to forget about the atrocities of the past. We were fortunate enough to have my mother accompany us on our journey to Poland in 2016. Then she went back to Poland and Israel in 2019. She is an international speaker at the Holocaust Memorial Center in Farmington Hills, MI as well as in Poland and in Israel. Her oral history can be viewed on the USC Shoah Foundation website. She can also be seen on *Portraits of Honor* at the Holocaust Memorial Center or online at www.portraitsofhonor.org. She is featured in Monni Must's book *Living Witnesses—Faces of the Holocaust*. She can be seen in *The Detroit News* (May 13, 2019), *Detroit Free Press* (May 13, 2019), *Detroit Jewish News* (April 2019), *The Jerusalem Post* (April 2019), *The Jewish News* (May 14, 2019), *The Japan Times, Yahoo News, Sun Sentinnel, The Israel National News*, in the Taiwan newspaper and Portuguese newspaper, on the FIDF websites, and more. She can be heard on a radio podcast on *Frontier Lines* and on the Mitch Albom podcast. She can be seen on *NBC News* and on the *Martha MacCallum Show* on *Fox News* (May, 2019).

This book is also dedicated to my Aunt Felicia Shloss. She was always educating others about the Holocaust at the Holocaust Memorial Centers in Michigan and Florida. She would have loved to have come on this journey with our family if she was still alive. Unfortunately, she passed away a week before we left for Poland in July 2016. She can be seen on *Portraits of Honor,* and on a videotape through Steven Spielberg.

Lastly, this book is dedicated to my beautiful children Michelle, Joshua and Kelsey. I wanted to make sure they had this resource and hopefully one day they will take their family on this journey.

Lori Klisman Ellis

"A woman of miracles. A story of survival and faith. Sophie is someone who, despite the horror she endured, still believes that miracles saved her."

~Friends of Israel Defense Forces

Letter From Anne Klisman, Sophie's Daughter-in-law

Sophie is a woman whose mantra is "you have to have hope." This has carried her through the holocaust. It has allowed her to be able to love again, recreate a family life after losing almost everyone in her family, and kept her well balanced. She is a role model for positive thinking and being satisfied with what you have.

Here is what I have observed as unique about Sophie Klisman. As her daughter-in-law, I observed and experienced her commitment to her family and to her work, share great love with her grandchildren, and later care for her husband as he battled Alzheimer Disease for more than 10 years. She did this with dignity, constantly showing kindness and a most positive attitude. I never heard her complain. She always had a smile and showed affection to the love of her life.

All the above being said, the following is where Sophie truly amazed me. Today's world has the buzzword for "lifelong learning." And at 85, Sophie, who had always been reticent to share her Holocaust story, began a new journey as a survivor speaker at the Holocaust Memorial Center. Yes, at 85, Sophie took the plunge into public speaking and teaching the lesson of kindness and hope to the youth of today.

As a docent myself, I have watched her take on an audience of up to 135 young people and mesmerize them with her story without projecting rage or hate, but with an emphasis for the importance of having hope and remaining positive. Every time she speaks, the students, along with their teachers, engulf and hug her when she is finished.

Sophie is remarkable. At 89, she has become one of the best teachers I know. To positively impact her audience, often filled with students who do not have the easiest of lives and be able to encourage them toward success with her words, "look, I went through horrible times, but I made a wonderful life and so can you," is truly helping to achieve the Jewish mitzvah of repairing the world. Sophie Klisman is remarkable.

Lori Klisman Ellis

Letter From Her Granddaughter

Sophie Klisman makes an impact in the Jewish community by speaking to groups at the Holocaust Memorial Center and sharing her story. Sophie paints a picture for her audience, vividly placing them in her shoes, allowing them to feel her fear growing up as a Jew, and provides them with a narrative of the challenges it took to survive the war. She provides an understanding for the importance of culture and community and leaves her audience with takeaways for building a better tomorrow.

Sophie makes an impact in the general community by providing a sense of family and belonging for her neighbors. She lives in a community with several widows and every night she brings chairs outside and invites her neighbors to join her for an evening of conversation and cookies. Some neighbors she knows, others she doesn't, and she invites them to come and go as they please so that they are never alone. She has built a subdivision of friends and most recently she stayed with one of these neighbors to assist in helping her recover from surgery.

Sophie is a member of the Holocaust Memorial Center where she volunteers as a speaker and attends fundraisers. She is also actively involved with fundraisers for the Friends of the Israeli Defense Forces. Previously, she was a member of local synagogues, involved in Sharit Ha-Platah (a group for Holocaust survivors), and a member of the B'nai Brith Women's Einstein Chapter.

Sophie is courageous. When she speaks at the Holocaust Memorial Center, she takes the time to comfort those who come to hear her speak. There have been several occasions where members of her audience have cried while hearing her story and they'll ask her questions about their own life. In these moments, Sophie is able to remove herself from the memories of her horrific childhood to comfort them and reassure them while they're scared. Sophie is supportive. Many of her close friends have recently passed away and Sophie takes the time to call her friends' children, ask about what they've been up to, offer her support and reminisce in memories of their parents. Sophie is altruistic. Every day she takes a walk in her subdivision in order to say hello and check in on her neighbors.

Sophie's most outstanding achievement is becoming an educator. As a child and into adulthood, Sophie had dreams of a career as a teacher but, due to the war, was unable to complete her schooling and attend college to become certified as a teacher. Over the last few years, she increased her involvement with the Holocaust Memorial Center to actively educate today's youth about the dangers of anti-Semitism and teach them the path to a better tomorrow. At 89 years old she is fulfilling her lifelong dream.

Sophie's legacy is providing hope for generations of Jews to come. She knows that every Jewish person has a story to tell and understands that not every Jew is capable of sharing their story. She was recently recorded sharing her story of survival and will forever be a permanent part of the Holocaust Memorial Museum. At 87 years old, Sophie traveled back to her hometown of Lodz, Poland, to put up a tombstone for her parents' and siblings' unmarked graves. She has taken on the task of speaking for those who cannot speak for themselves and is living her life to honor the lives of those she cared about.

Sophie exemplifies a long-term commitment to Tikkun Olan by volunteering her time with both Jews and non-Jews. Her physical involvement has allowed her to share compassion in reassuring today's youth that they can make a difference. She has been there to reinforce a look of encouragement and she has facilitated conversations about change. She is involved, and she has had a hand in molding our next generation.

After Sophie's husband and best friend passed away (both of whom were Holocaust survivors), she made the decision, at 84 years old, to make her life's work teaching others the danger of anti-Semitism and the importance of acceptance and love. She put her fear of reliving her past aside, knowing in the not-so-distant future there won't be anyone left to share their story, and has been actively involved in reshaping the world.

Sophie Tajch Klisman and her sister Felicia at a displaced persons camps in Germany, circa 1947.

4,456 Miles

Table of Contents

Dedication 3

Letter From Anne Klisman............................. 5

Letter From Her Granddaughter 6

Acknowledgments 12

Foreword... 13

Introduction... 15

Part I: Pre-World War II & The Start Of The Ghetto 17
Chapter 1   Life In Piotrkow/Trybunalski, Poland
Chapter 2   Facts About Lodz, Poland
Chapter 3   Map Of Poland

Part II: War Time / Holocaust.......................... 23
Chapter 4   The War Broke Out
Chapter 5   Where In Poland Were My Parents From?
Chapter 6   Insight Into Bernard Klisman
Chapter 7   The Parallel Lives Between
               Two Pairs Of Sisters
Chapter 8   Summary Of Oral Testimony On
               Sophie Klisman & Felicia Shloss

Part III: Liberation / Post WWII 57
Chapter 9   Liberation April 14, 1945
Chapter 10   After The Concentration Camps &
               Into The DP Camps
Chapter 11   Life After The War
Chapter 12   From Tragedy To Triumph

Part IV: Poland Here We Come—70 Years Later......... 70
Chapter 13   How My Interest In Poland Began
Chapter 14   Our Journey To Poland

Part V: Genealogy Research & Notes.................. 80
Chapter 15   Highlights Of Email Correspondences
               With The Genealogist

Part VI: On Traveling To Poland In 2016 84
Chapter 16   Daily Diary/Blogs
Chapter 17   Mediums & Spiritual Posts

Part VII: Life After The Journey 152
Chapter 18   Life After The Journey To Poland
Chapter 19   A Speaker At The Holocaust Center
Chapter 20   Where Do We Go From Here?
Chapter 21   How Can An Ordinary Citizen Make An
             Impact In Eradicating Anti-Semitism?

Part VIII: Finding New Family 164
Chapter 22   Online Groups
Chapter 23   The Family Is Growing
Chapter 24   The Family Continues To Grow

**Part IX: Preparing For The
2019 FIDF Mission To Poland/Israel** 171
Chapter 25   Mom Is Going On An Incredible Mission

**Part X: Public Relations
Information On Sophie Klisman** 175
Chapter 26   Newspapers, The News, Videos,
             And Radio Stations

Part XI: 84th Infantry Soldier Meets Survivor 179
Chapter 27   The Long Anticipated Reunion

**Part XII: Poland & Israel
FIDF Mission May 2–May 10, 2019** 185
Chapter 28   Sophie Klisman's Trifold Mission:
             Educate, Eradicate Hate & Get Closure
Chapter 29   Reflections Of The Mission

Part XIII: Senior Olympics 191
Chapter 30   Senior Olympic Gold

**Appendix A: Key Points From
Books On The Holocaust**................................ 192
- Insight Into Surviving The Concentration Camps: *Man's Search For Meaning* By Viktor E. Frankl
- Relating The Holocaust To The book *When Bad Things Happen To Good People* By Rabbi Harold Kushner
- Facts About The Holocaust From *In Broad Daylight: The Secret Procedures Behind The Holocaust By Bullets* By Father Patrick Desbois

Appendix B: Family Ancestry 203
- The Tree Of Life—Ellis/Klisman Family Tree
- The Family Tree
- Family Stories
- Resources From *It's All Relative* By A. J. Jacobs & From Lori Ellis

Appendix C: DNA Information...................... 218

Appendix D: Creating Your Own Trip To Poland..... 222
- Poland Itinerary
- Travel Tips
- Sampling Of Sites
- Hotels

Appendix E: Photo Gallery........................... 229
- Early Photos
- Family Photos
- FIDF Photos From The 2019 Mission

Conclusion 248

Bibliography.. 249

Acknowledgments

I met with Zieva Konvisser, the first person to give my mother "a voice." She helped my mother open up in order to do an interview for the Holocaust Memorial Center. When we met, I shared information on my book. She gave me her interpretation and she thought that my journey to Poland awakened me as being a second generation survivor. For my whole life, I could not relate to other second generation survivors. I felt as if I had a different upbringing than them and in a way I did. My brother and I were sheltered from the stories of the Holocaust. My parents protected and shielded us from hearing these atrocities. Now I want to share what I learned for my future generations.

So thank you to Zieva Konvisser for taking time out of your busy day to give me your suggestions, support, and guidance. In essence this book is an oxymoron. I did experience a "Spiritual Awakening" but at the same time my mother experienced closure. I am going to call this book *4, 456 Miles: A Survivor's Search for Closure—Awakening Her Daughter's Search For Understanding the Holocaust.*

Thank you to Feiga Weiss for providing me with websites, books, support, and guidance. You were the catalyst I needed to get my research in the right direction.

Thank you to Esther Gold for travel tips.

Thank you to Lou Okell at Arkett Publishing for your assistance, endless patience, and helping to make the book beautiful.

Thank you to my mother for finally sharing her story and educating the world on the Holocaust. My family and I are in awe of your bravery, positive attitude, kindness, love, and caring disposition. Thanks also to my family for their support in my endeavor to learn and write about the Holocaust.

Foreword

Sophie Tajch Klisman shares her poignant and harrowing personal journey as a survivor of the Lodz ghetto, Auschwitz-Birkenau Concentration and Extermination Camp, Bergen-Belsen Camp, and Salzwedel Camp. Trauma has severely impacted Sophie's life but she learns it is possible to have a long and fulfilling life after the trauma. As Sophie stated "I am living two lives, a horrific one in the past and a beautiful one in the present." *4,456 Miles...* is a cathartic book that shares Sophie's mantra of "hope" to anyone facing hardships in their life.

Sophie created a new life in the USA after the war by hiding the deep, dark secret of her past life from her children and colleagues. She along with her husband never spoke about the Holocaust. With the encouragement of her daughter-in-law she started sharing her story at the Holocaust Memorial Center. Her daughter encouraged Sophie and her family to return to Poland in 2016 to put up a tombstone in the exact spot where the Tajch family was buried in Lodz, Poland, which added some closur to her life.

When Sophie was selected to be a Holocaust speaker in Poland and Israel for the Mission of the Friends of the Israel Defense Forces in May 2019, she finally achieved the missing pieces of her life: closure, safety, and peace. The soldiers of the Israel Defense Forces marched into Auschwitz-Birkenau with her while she shared her harrowing story. She survived the war and was recognized around the world as a true hero. She never needs to hide her story again! Her family and the world are proud of her accomplishments.

As if that was not enough, another magical moment happened. A 95-year-old man named Doug Harvey, a GI from the 84th infantry, read her story on the cover of the Detroit news and stated he was a liberator of one of her concentration camps. They reunited 75 years later. She said "he was an angel who gave me back my life."

Sophie's daughter, Lori Klisman Ellis shares her recent search for understanding the Holocaust as she traces her mother's story back to Poland and, in the process, discovers her responsibility as a second generation survivor to carry on her mother's legacy and give "hope" to others by bearing witness to the Holocaust. Her passion is to educate the world on the dangers of hatred, prejudice, and anti-Semitism. Now is a critical time in our history to share this message as anti-Semitism is on the rise!

Lori Klisman Ellis

Within Lori's search of the Holocaust she realizes a missing part of her and her family's life was not knowing names of people in her family. She was missing her "Family Tree." The Tree of Life was chopped down to the stump. After much research her tree is blooming with new leaves and flowers. It has been resurrected and by sharing names of family and information about them, Lori and her family are watering their tree, watching it bloom and keeping the memory of those that perished alive. There is a how to guide on growing your own tree, doing DNA research and watching your family grow!

—Jeff Ellis

Introduction

Can you imagine living a life in a world surrounded by chaos, darkness, and terror? As you will soon learn, Zysla was born into a loving family and at ten years of age her life as well as her family's life took on a drastic change. She endured years of hell and torture in the confines of the Lodz ghetto and three concentration camps. Zysla, the youngest in her family, along with her older sister, Fajga, would be the only two people in her immediate and extended family to survive the darkest, most horrific time in history. You will learn about her life prior to the war, during World War II, and after her liberation. Zysla shares her story of hope, miracles, and determination to survive the Holocaust. It is also a story of recreating a new life, a new name, and a new family in the USA.

Once Zysla arrived in the US, the Holocaust became a deep, dark secret that was hidden for over 70 years. Eventually, with encouragement, the story slowly was shared at the Holocaust Memorial Center in Michigan. With love and support, Zysla's family accompanied her back to her Polish roots. Follow her journey to Poland in 2016 as well as her return to Poland and Israel in 2019.

Seventy-five years later, Zysla a/k/a Sophie Tajch Klisman found closure, safety, and peace with the help of her family and the Israeli soldiers she met. Magical moments happened during these trips.

Here are some of her reactions: "My life has changed forever!" On meeting Doug Harvey of the US 84th Infantry: "Never in my wildest dreams would I have imagined meeting you. After 75 years we reunite. You are my hero, my angel. You and the other soldiers from the 84th infantry were angels jumping off their tanks and trucks and opening up the gate of Salzwedel camp. If it wasn't for you, Doug, I would not have had a life."

Now Sophie is living her life filled with zest, love, and passion. She is educating people within the US as well as internationally on the dangers of hatred and prejudice. She is winning gold medals in the Senior Olympics. Sophie is an inspiration to all and she exemplifies kindness and love.

Lori Klisman Ellis

Piotrkow/Trybunalski, Poland (wikimedia)

Part I: Pre-World War II and The Start Of The Ghetto

Chapter 1 Life In Piotrkow/Trybunalski, Poland

Zysla Tajch wondered if she would feel safe going back to her home town in Piotrkow in 2016? "Let's just go in and out of the city quickly. We do not need to walk around the town."

"Mom, if we are going to Poland we should see where you grew up. Can you imagine retracing your roots and going back to the synagogue you used to go to as a child with your family?"

I started wondering too if there would be any anti-Semitism in Poland. Would we stick out like a sore thumb?

Liba Rozrazoska, my grandmother, was the daughter of Zysla and Berek Rozrazowska. She was 22 years old when she married Icek Berek Tajch (my grandfather). They were married in Piotrkow, Poland. Between 1917 and 1929 they had five children—Moszek, Israel (Srulek), Fajga, Estera (who passed away from an illness at approximately the age of 9), and Zysla (my mother). Zysla was born on July 6, 1929 in Piotrkow, Poland.

According to my mother, Zylsa Tajch, she had a loving family. Liba was a stay at home mother which was typical of women in that era. Her husband Icek Berek was a shoe maker. He worked long hours to help provide food and shelter for their family. My mother has memories of her mother and father taking her to the park and buying her cookies. She played ball outside in the courtyard with her friends and siblings. Life was difficult but good. Zysla and her sister Fajga attended an all girl's Jewish school. Zysla completed four grades with dobry (good) marks on her report card.

Piotrkow was established in the 13th century. Initially Jews were not allowed to live there. In the 16th century the Jewish community was established in Piotrkow. There were a few Polish nobleman that rented homes to Jews and thus a small Jewish community was established. In the 17th century there was a pogrom in Piotrkow and the Jewish community was nearly destroyed. There were fires and destruction to synagogues. By the 18th century Jews were told they had to pay higher taxes than non-Jews. During the 19th century Piotrkow was under the control of Russia. Social aid and welfare were provided to the Jewish citizens. There were Synagogues in town, one being the "Great Synagogue" which we visited in 2016. After the war it was transformed into a library. Before World War II, almost one-third of the population of Piotrkow was Jewish. Some Jewish families were affluent and some were poor. It was one of the oldest towns in Poland. Piotrkow's Jewish community dealt mostly with commerce and manufacturing of textiles as well as glass products and wood. Many factories were owned by Jews.

The war broke out on September 1, 1939. Anti-Semitism was on the rise prior to the war breaking out. Derogatory comments about the Jews were on the rise. Hitler was brainwashing soldiers to hate the Jews. People needed scapegoats for poor economic conditions and they blamed the Jews for controlling the banks and other industries. Hitler began stealing the symbol of swastikas and the arm salute from other countries and nationalities. Hatred against the Jews was ingrained into children at a young age. Germany persuaded other neighboring countries to buy into anti-Semitism.

By 1939 the Tajch family was already in Lodz. They relocated because it was a bigger city and had greater opportunities. There were no cars at the time so they must have been transported by horse drawn buggies. That 16 mile distance from Piotrkow to Lodz must have felt like they were moving to another state.

Germany occupied the city of Piotrkow on September 5, 1939. One thousand Jews were killed in the beginning of the month and two thousand Jews escaped to neighboring areas. The Nazis created the Piotrkow ghetto which had fences and barbed wire. Thousands of Jews were forced into an approximately one square mile area to live. They were told to bring a suitcase of their valuable possessions. Many were promised a better life if they willingly relocated. Most Jewish families did not know how horrific conditions would be. Life became very difficult for people. There was hardly any food and families were forced to share rooms with others they did not know. Many people began dying from disease and starvation.

During the very beginning of the war, there was some underground resistance in Piotrkow. Piotrkow was the first town to create a Jewish ghetto. The Nazis imprisoned around twenty five thousand Jews from Piotrkow and other nearby towns. Twenty-two thousand people were eventually sent to Treblinka, which was an extermination camp. The three thousand people who were not sent to Treblinka were sent to other concentration camps. Hardly anyone survived at that camp (only 26 survivors)! Five months later, the Jews in Lodz were sent to ghettos.

Lodz ghetto decree Jan. 24, 1940 (wikimedia)

Lori Klisman Ellis

This is the bridge my mother walked on daily in the Lodz ghetto. This image is used with permission from Nancy Hartman at the Holocaust Memorial Holocaust Museum on September 8, 2019.

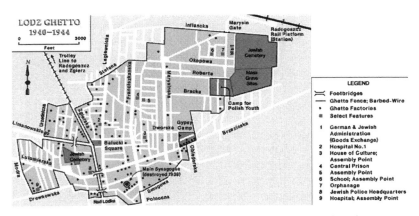

This photo is of the Lodz ghetto 1940-1944. This image is used with consent from the US Holocaust Memorial Museum. The model was duplicated by a prisoner, Leon Jakubowicz.

4,456 Miles

Chapter 2 Facts About Lodz, Poland

"It will be difficult to go back to Lodz because this is where my beautiful mother, father, and one brother perished in the ghetto. I can't believe we will view the tombstone we just erected for the Tajch family!"

- Lodz was Poland's third largest city in Europe.
- Lodz was an industrial center prior to the war.
- It is located 75 miles southwest of Warsaw, Poland.
- Lodz held the second largest Jewish community prior to WWII.
- In 1931 Lodz had a total population of 604,629 and 202,696 were Jews.
- Germany invaded Lodz September 1, 1939 and renamed it Litzmannstadt.
- In February, 1940 a ghetto was established which housed 160,000 Jews. This was more than a third of the city's population.
- Another document stated 200,000 Jews passed through this ghetto and a mere 844 survived until the liberation.
- Villagers of Lodz were forced by the police to put up the barbed wire and create the Lodz ghetto.
- The ghetto was divided into three parts and had two major roads. There were bridges constructed over the two roads connecting the three sections of the ghetto. My mother remembers walking on those bridges. When we came back to Lodz she looked for the bridges but they were all destroyed after the war.
- Factories were established in the ghetto and the Jewish prisoners were forced labor workers. The merchandise was sent to the soldiers in Germany.
- There was minimal food, no pay, and no running water or sewers.
- More than 20% of the ghetto's prisoner's died including my grandmother Liba, my grandfather Icek Berek, my uncle Moszek and thousands more. They died due to starvation and disease. It was August 25, 1941 when Liba perished. Eleven months later on July 17, 1942 Icek Berek perished. Two months later their son Moszek (Moishe) died on September 21, 1942. This must have been the most painful and devastating thing to witness!
- Some of the Jews from the Lodz ghetto were deported to Chelmno concentration camp.
- The elderly, sick, and young children were killed.

The remaining Jewish population such as my mother Sophie, my Aunt Felicia, and my Uncle Israel were deported five years later to Auschwitz-Birkenau concentration camp. My mother felt the reason why she survived the selection at Auschwitz was because she was kept in the Lodz ghetto for five years. Those years allowed her to become older and grow. At Auschwitz, if a person was not a certain height or sixteen years of age, they were sent to the gas chambers immediately. Fortunately my mother made it through the selection. *(More information will be provided on this topic.)*

During my family's visit to Lodz, Poland in 2016 we had an opportunity to see a cosmopolitan city with a vibrant night life, outdoor cafes, the Manufacktura mall, hotels, the Survivor Park, the Radegast Railway Station, the Lodz cemetery, Izrael Poznanski's tombstone as well as his Palace, and more. We toured the popular street called Ulica Piotrkowska. My mother was interested to know if the bridges were still erect but they were taken down after the liquidation of the ghetto. My mother said nothing looked familiar. As a youth she merely saw the confines of the ghetto.

(Information from the Holocaust Memorial Center in Washington D.C.)

Chapter 3 Map Of Poland

4,456 Miles

Part II: War Time / Holocaust

Chapter 4 The War Broke Out

Germany attacked Poland on September 1, 1939.

Newspaper.com

The Soviet Union also joined the Germans in attacking Poland. Not only was this occurring in Poland, but the transportation of Jews was occurring all over Europe. According to research by en.wikipedia.org/wiki/holocaust_trains, the Germans were invading Belgium, Bulgaria, Bohemia and Moravia, Greece, Italy, Romania, Scandinavia, Switzerland, Slovakia, Sweden, France, Hungary, Netherlands, and Poland.

In Belgium there was resistance on trains to the concentration camps. A fire was purposely started and as a result of this 118 Jews escaped but unfortunately several others were shot and some others were recaptured.

In Slovakia the leaders of that country could not wait to get rid of the Jewish population, so they paid the SS 40 million Reichsmarks (RM). It was approximately 500 RM's per Jew.

In Switzerland, the Germans needed their tunnels and bridges so they did not invade that area. The Jews were still there.

In Scandinavia (Norway) half the Jews escaped to Sweden where they were safe.

Sweden was a neutral country. The leaders of Sweden let the Jews know in advance that the Germans were coming for them, so many were provided with a boat to leave. When they returned, they were welcomed back and their property was returned to them.

In Romania, most Jews died in transport since it was 7 days without food, water or fresh air. The Germans hammered the windows shut with planks so there was no way to get air or escape.

In Greece, Italy, Bohemia, and Moravia most Jews were sent to the Concentration camps and perished there.

There were protests by Rabbis and Priests in Bulgaria after Jews were deported to concentration camps. None of the Jews were released, however they prevented 49,000 more Jews from being deported. The King was not good to the Jews that remained in Bulgaria and he imposed racial restrictions on them such as giving up their money and possessions.

In the Netherlands all the Jews were sent to the concentration camps and only 4.86% survived.

In France, where my mother's Aunt Sheindl was, the Red Cross protested sending the Jews to camps, but there were still 76,000 deported. Most of the Jews from Paris were sent to Drancy Internment Camp and from there to Auschwitz-Birkenau Concentration and Extermination Camp. Unfortunately, there are no records of my mother's Aunt Sheindl from the International Tracing Society (ITS). In 2014 France National Railway Company took responsibility for their part in the mass transit of Jews and paid $60 million worth of compensation to the US Holocaust survivors.

Poland had the greatest number of Jews deported. In September, 1939, Germany took over the Polish railways. They killed the Polish people working at the rail stations. They switched to a German Transport Authority. The Germans also renamed the streets in Poland which caused some confusion. Jews in Poland were deported to many concentration and extermination camps such as Chelmno, Treblinka, Auschwitz-Birkenau, and others.

Chapter 5 Where In Poland Were My Parents From?

Life began in a loving, safe environment that quickly transitioned to inhumane living conditions.

Where in the world was **Zysla/Zosia Tajch** a/k/a **Sophie Klisman** from?

Zysla was born in Piotrkow and moved at a young age to Lodz. Once in Lodz the family was relocated from their apartment and forced to move into the Lodz ghetto. She along with her family had poor living conditions. There was a ration on food, so family members were starving. The goal of the Nazis was to exterminate all Jews via starvation. This way they did not have to waste bullets or get blood on their hands. In the camps, "the German system was to give thirty people food for ten and the ten who fought the hardest stayed alive." (The 84th Infantry Division Book, page 244). Therefore, they were provided one slice of bread to last the entire day and watered down soup in a bowl without silverware. Zysla also was forced to live with unfamiliar families in cramped conditions. This lasted five years. Many people perished there including her parents and one brother, Moszek.

From there, my mother, her sister Fajga and brother Israel were the only survivors of their family from the ghetto. They were forced to go to the Radegast Railway Station and were transported to Auschwitz-Birkenau. They were there for approximately 15 days. From there they were once again transported by cattle cars to Bergen-Belsen. Females were separated from the males, so Fajga and Zysla never realized that their brother Israel was also sent to Bergen-Belsen. Zysla stated that even if they were to have run into him, they would not have recognized one another because their heads were shaved and they lost so much weight that they started to look like skeletons. Tragically, they never saw their brother again. Both Zysla and Fajga were eventually transported with hundreds of other people in a small, overcrowded cattle car to Salzwedel. People continued to cry, scream, faint, and even die on their journey to Salzwedel. Salzwedel was in operation from late July or early August 1944 to April 1945. Liberation from the women's satellite camp finally occurred on April 14th, 1945.

According to documents that I read from the United States Holocaust Memorial Museum, Encyclopedia of Camps, and Ghettos

This is a photo of a crematorium in Auschwitz-Birkenau Concentration and Extermination Camp. Photo taken by Ellen Bushman

Roll call in the camps (from meeroverdeholocaust.nl)

4,456 Miles

from 1933–1945 there were over 20,000 camps and ghettos. They spread from France, Belgium, the Netherlands in the west, to Poland and the USSR in the east; from Norway and the Baltic states in the north to Romania, Yugoslavia and to Greece. The camps and ghettos were also in North African Colonies.

Auschwitz-Birkenau was one of the most notorious camps. Within the first twenty minutes of arriving at Auschwitz, most of the people were sent to the crematorium. A mere two out of ten people made it through the selection process. Miraculously, some of the family made it through the selection process. Zysla and her sister Fajga Tajch and Israel Tajch were sent to Auschwitz. My father Benek Klisman was also sent there, although the sisters and Israel did not know Benek at that time. My mother and her sister believed they arrived in August of 1944 for approximately 15 days. The survived with was one slice of bread and watered down soup, hardly any sleep, and brutal conditions. My father was there for several months and by a miracle he survived this horrific camp.

In less than five years, 1.3 million people were killed in the Auschwitz-Birkenau camp and over 90% were European Jews. 90% of Jewish inmates were gassed to death. This camp was located outside a small Polish city called Oswiecim. Some Jewish families lived in Oswiecim before the war. People were evacuated from this town and the SS soldiers took over their homes. The soldiers and their families had an affluent lifestyle there.

On April 27, 1940 there was an order issued to build this notorious camp. Auschwitz had a 49% mortality rate. More than one half of all inmates in Auschwitz were Jews. Jews were ranked low and were treated the harshest. During June 1940–January 1945, the SS soldiers and Nazis made over $60 million reichsmarks in profit by exploiting inmates in Auschwitz.

One of the ways to survive Auschwitz was by "organizing" which meant stealing and smuggling anything of value that could be exchanged or bartered for privileges or food. Food was rationed severely there. Another way to survive was to stay out of the radar of the SS soldiers. When working close to the soldiers, they would physically abuse their victims sometimes because they were not working fast enough, doing their job good enough, or for no apparent reason.

During all the camps, my mother recalled the constant roll calls. These occurred at the beginning of the day and at the end of the day and sometimes in the middle of the night. They lasted for two hours. I saw where the SS soldiers transferred the prisoners during

Bunk Beds in Auschwitz-Birkenau Concentration and Extermination Camps. Photo taken by Ellen Bushman

This is a communal toilet or outhouse used in Auschwitz-Birkenau Concentration and Extermination camps. Photo taken by Ellen Bushman.

roll call. They made them get up and walk to a separate destination just to add fatigue to their weakened bodies. My mother did not know why this was done so frequently. She said after working shifts in the middle of the night the SS would wake them up to do roll call. The reason this was done was to add torment and fatigue! Prisoners worked shifts of 12 hours a day. Mom shared how horrible it was to be a teenager who required more sleep and to have to be sleep deprived. Exhaustion took over. Compound exhaustion with no food made it impossible for the majority of prisoners to survive. Only one or two free Sundays a month were provided, however they still had to do roll calls and jobs around the bunkers. So that only gave them a few hours to themselves.

There were very few prisoners that escaped Auschwitz although there were some resistant groups in Auschwitz. There were suicides on the barbed wire when victims could no longer endure the torture and suffering. For most it was impossible to escape because the Nazis had machine guns and rifles and many were in towers constantly watching over them. Some Jewish inmates were assigned to watch over the prisoners. They were some of the toughest and cruelest people. They were given special privileges for doing this.

My father was tattooed but my mother and aunt were not. The workers could not keep up with the large influx of people coming to Auschwitz. The gas chambers and crematorium at Auschwitz could kill 2,000 people at one time. It was a miracle that anyone survived. Horrible medical procedures were carried out at this camp and others. Shockingly only 630 SS soldiers were apprehended and tried out of 7,000 SS personnel.

Bergen-Belsen was another camp my mother, Aunt Fajga (Felicia) and Uncle Israel were sent to. Once again, Sophie and Aunt Felicia were never aware that their brother was also at Bergen-Belsen. Men and women were separated. The whole time they thought he perished in Auschwitz.

Upon entering Bergen-Belsen the sign read "Lasciate Ognisperanza" which translates to "Abandon all hope." What despair they must have felt upon entering another horrific camp. This camp was initially set up to be a detention camp. It was established in 1943. On June 29, 1943 the initial name of the camp was changed to "Aufenthaltslager Bergen-Belsen" because it was to be in accordance with the Geneva Convention and to be open for inspection by International Commissions. Movies were shown to the prisoners only when the Red Cross came to the camps to inspect them. The SS Soldiers made certain prisoners dress up

Some prisoners were killed by the death squad. They were sent to this brick wall and they were shot. This occurred in Auschwitz-Birkenau Concentration and Extermination Camp. Photo taken by Ellen Bushman

Bergen-Belsen Concentration Camp. (from Scrapbookpages.com)

and played instruments as if they were part of an orchestra. Other prisoners were told to play soccer. The Red Cross left thinking the prisoners were treated humanely. As soon as the Red Cross left they were once again treated inhumanely.

Sophie and Aunt Felicia estimated they arrived in Bergen-Belsen in September of 1944. They stated they were there 4–5 weeks. In the autumn of 1944 this camp was built. It did not have bunkers to sleep on, only the floor with some straw. They slept in tents. There were no blankets or mattresses. When it rained it poured on them. There was no heat or air conditioning. It would rain and pour through the roof as they would lay on the ground. They were cold, wet, famished, and exhausted. Females from Poland were sent there and some worked in the armament industry. My mother stated there was not a lot of work for them at this location.

This was a place where Jewish prisoners were to be exchanged for Germans interned in Western countries. In reality, very few prisoners were exchanged. Not only were Mom and Aunt Felicia there, but also Anne Frank and her sister Margot. Surprisingly at Bergen-Belsen some of the guards allowed prisoners pens and pencils and papers. This is where some wrote diaries. Unfortunately Anne Frank and her sister died one month before this camp was liberated. Mom and Aunt Felicia never met Anne Frank. My mother and aunt were once again transported to another camp; this time it was Salzwedel.

Salzwedel was located in Germany. At the end of July or beginning of August an External camp to Neuengamme was built just for women. The Polte Company had a Wires and Metal works factory called Salzwedel prior to WW 2. When the war started the factory produced ammunition for the infantry. They also produced anti-aircraft batteries. The request was for 5,600 forced laborers but they only received 1,520 Jewish women initially. Eventually 3,000 women were transported to this camp. They were mainly Jewish women. The women lived in barracks on a fertilizer factory on a street called Gardelegener.

My mother believes she was at this camp for 9 months. She worked in a munitions factory from 6:00 p.m. to 6:00 a.m. Women were forced to work a 12 hour shift. She had to fill bullet casings. At times the machine would misfire and workers would get killed. There was not a lot of sleeping during the day. They were woken up for two hour long roll calls in order to create more exhaustion, humiliation, and intimidation. My mother became extremely exhausted from no sleep. She eventually became ill and collapsed.

Lori Klisman Ellis

This photo is from the 1990's showing the former munitions factory in Salzwedel. Sophie recalls having to work underground. (Archives of Neuengamme Concentration Camp Memorial 1990-9430)

(Archives Neuengamme Concentration Camp Memorial, 1981-0114 showing the factory of Messap and Jastram on the grounds of Neuengamme Concentration Camp 1943 or 1944) *In the second half of the war, armaments production became the main focus of work in the concentration camp. The prisoners of the Neuengamme main camp were employed in the armaments factories of the Jastram and Messap Companies (Like in the photo), the Neuengamme metal works (Walther-Werke) and the factory of the SS owned company Deutshe Ausrustungswerke (DAW). However, only men prisoners were working in the armaments production in the main camp. Zysla and Fajga were working in a subcamp of Neuengamme in Hamburg, Germany called Salzwedel. According to my mother's memory, the set up or logistics of this factory was the same as the factory she worked in. Note: Once again a prisoner on the left has an X on the back of his work garment. This was the target area to shoot the prisoner if he stepped away from his work or was not doing his job.*

4,456 Miles

My Aunt tried to hold her up during roll call and during the walk to work. My mother just collapsed. One SS woman guard told her to go back to the bunk and rest. She was thrilled. Within a few minutes she fell asleep. After a few minutes a different SS woman guard without a heart, started swearing at her and beating her to near death. She was forced to walk to the factory while being beaten on the head the whole way. Upon finally getting to the factory Felicia was shocked to see her covered with blood. Felicia tried to clean her face, and when the supervisor left them to do their work, she found a back room and had my mother lie down on the floor and sleep. When other supervisors went back to check on the workers, my mother's name was not on the list to work that day, so no one expected her to be at work. After the shift was over, her sister woke her up and had her walk back with the rest of them to their bunk. My mother said that little amount of sleep she had was a miracle and helped her feel better.

My mother does not recall any medical assistance at this camp. However, one document I read by Edith Levinson, a former prison nurse stated the SS guards selected her to be a nurse at Salzwedel. She had no medical training but she had several doctors in her family so it was not foreign to her. She was supervised by an SS member who was a registered nurse, but did not treat patients. Edith was instructed not to have more than seven or eight sick people in the "sick bay" at one time. Also, anyone with a fever under 39 degrees centigrade (102.2 degrees F) had to work. Edith said the worst part of her job was deciding who was so sick and emaciated and then she had to send them away (which meant they were going to die). She spoke to a physician from Salzwedel who was a civilian and a member of the party. He stated there are some French people here (possibly workers that fix machines) and asked them for some medication. She got some drugs for a headache or fever. She hid the medication and used it when necessary. (Information came from Translation "Salzwedel" page 5.) This makes sense now when my Aunt Felicia spoke about my mother receiving a green pill when she was ill. She was in the "sick bay" for three days and thank goodness made it out alive. Bergen-Belsen and Auschwitz were concentration camps without a "sick bay." If a person were to say they were ill, they would have been killed or sent away which meant death.

This was the location where the 84th Infantry, 9th US army came and liberated my mother, her sister, as well as 2,998 other female inmates. My mother stated she will never forget that day on April 14, 1945. In the beginning of April is when the victims started hearing explosions and gun fire and my Aunt said if they can hold on a little longer they were hopeful they would be liberated. Upon liberation the Mayor ordered the people in the town to feed the victims. So they ran out the gates and got food, but my mother just wanted to get sleep. When Aunt Felicia came back she brought my mother some food. Some of the soldiers gave the victims candy, crackers, or whatever they had with them. Several liberated women died from over eating or from the brutality of the camps after liberation. The fortunate survivors were told to eat a small amount in order to eventually stretch their stomachs. The women worked with dieticians and were given a lot of liquid and gradually increased the amount of solid food, in order to stretch their stomach. The survivors were going to Displaced Person (DP) camps and tried to integrate into a normal life.

Where in the world was **Benek Klisman** a/k/a/ Bernie Klisman from?

Bernie was born in Sosnowiec, Poland; however his brothers and sister were from Zarki, Poland. In 1939 Germany invaded his home town of Sosnowiec. The Klisman family was forced to be in Srodula which was a ghetto in Sosnowiec. Srodula is a district of Sosnowiec and the Germans established a ghetto there.

Bernie was picked up daily from his home and was forced to clean the streets and do road repair work. He had to clean the Police stations and offices that were occupied by the Germans. In 1940 groups were taken to adjacent cities such as Katovitz and Koenig which were resort areas. He had to demolish large buildings with hand tools. Since he was not familiar with the use of hand tools it took him longer to demolish buildings. As a result of this he was beaten regularly. He also had to dig large holes, which were made into swimming pools for officers to use. In 1942 Bernie was taken to Parzymiechy, which was a farm community. From there he was transported to Annaberg in Saxony, Germany and did whatever work he was demanded to do.

By the summer of 1943 the Germans liquidated the ghetto in Srodula and transported 10,000 Jews beginning in August to **Auschwitz-Birkenau.** He was one of the young boys transported to Auschwitz but not until 1944. He was in Auschwitz for four months. He was forced to clean the streets, clean lavatories, and anything else asked of him. He received constant beatings because he could not work as hard as they wanted him to, because he was weakened by the hard work, lack of food, and beatings.

4,456 Miles

After Auschwitz he was sent to **Landsburg**, which is southwest of Bavaria, Germany. This is where the Germans had underground factories. Records indicated that Hitler was held prisoner at Landsburg back in 1924 for treason. Unfortunately, he was only there for 264 days. It is unreal to think how history would have been different if Hitler was in prison for life. There would have been six million additional survivors and millions of their heirs.

Next he was sent to **Dachau** and was finally liberated from there on April 29, 1945 by the US Seventh Army's 42nd and 45th Infantry divisions as well as the 20th Armored Division. They liberated approximately 32,000 prisoners.

After his liberation he went to a small town called **Feldmoching**. Feldmoching was located in the northern part of Bavaria, Germany. Many survivors stayed in a Displaced Person's camp in Feldmoching but my father stayed in a private home for a few weeks. This home was supported by the United States Army. After that stay the Jewish Community Council took over the support of him and others. He received dental care by a surgeon who removed the roots of broken teeth caused by the beatings from the SS Nazis.

In 1948 he was sent to a TB sanitarium in the foothills of the Bavarian Alps in Germany. This is where he was treated for apparently Tuberculosis. This place was called **Schloss-Elmau**.

Schloss-Elmau (wikimedia)

Chapter 6 Insight Into Bernard Klisman

In 1938, when Bernard was 15 years old he started working in the manufacture of boxes for jewelry and other precious items. He also completed seventh grade. He lived with his parents, six brothers, and one sister. The German occupation of Poland occurred in 1940. His education was halted. He was taken for forced labor and some of the jobs were in surrounding towns in Upper Silesia. That is where he did demolition, construction, and similar types of hard labor. In 1941 the Jews were forced into the ghetto and when the Germans liquidated the ghetto, people were sent to Auschwitz. Many people were killed while younger men and women were in a job that fit the German industrial purposes and sent to labor camps. Both of my father's parents were sent to Auschwitz and perished there.

Bernard Klisman c. 1995

Bernie went to a ghetto in a neighboring city and worked in a shirt manufacturing plant that supplied the German government. In 1942 he was sent to a labor camp in Parzymiechy. He did farm work there. The city had a natural inland lake, and being the home of the General, he and high officials used this lake for boating and swimming. The weather was becoming horribly cold in the fall. My father was forced to enter the pond, drain and clean it from all the debris that accumulated in the summer. He became very ill. He worked for many days in the cold and damp conditions. This is when my father thought he had pneumonia because he had a high fever and consistently coughed. There was no medicine for him and limited food and water. It was a miracle that he survived with pneumonia. The camp was liquidated in 1942.

After that my father was sent to Camp Annaberg. He was forced to work in a factory there. Then he was sent to Camp Landsberg where he was building a factory for the Messerschmitt airplane manufacturing company. This was high priority for the German government because they wanted to get the airplanes manufactured. This was very hard labor for my father and the other prisoners. They did a lot of construction, most of the time unloading cement and other building materials from trains. He only received a small piece of moldy bread for the whole day. When he was sick

4,456 Miles

and did not go to work bread was not provided, but merely watered down soup for the day. One time he was quite sick but decided to go to work because he didn't want to lose his piece of bread, but he could not perform the work as well as he was supposed to. He complained that he was too weak and the German supervisor attacked him and beat him severely. As a result of that beating he suffered a permanent partial sensorineural hearing loss in the left ear. The SS guards fractured his teeth. He was beaten over the head and other parts of the body until he lost consciousness. He was left on the ground and his fellow prisoners fortunately took him back to the barracks. He was still forced to do work. He went down to 80–90 pounds by the end of the war and he suffered from ulcers, which he was still being treated for after the war.

The Soviet army was getting close to this camp, so the Nazi soldiers forced them to relocate to a new camp, Dachau. My father remained at Dachau until his liberation day on April 24, 1945 (ten days after my mother and Aunt were liberated). This camp was so overcrowded and there was no work for them. The camp had so much unnatural dirt and sickening conditions. There was so much starvation there. He was so weak that he had to be taken to a hospital upon liberation and given liquid foods for a few weeks before he could start to learn to eat again. He had to learn how to walk again, as well as to be able to nourish himself.

Dachau became a Displaced Person camp and my father was there for a little while. Eventually he was moved to Feldmoching where he lived with a private family. Several weeks later, the UNRRA organized food supplies for former concentration camp inmates and this is where he received medical care. He found out most of his relatives were dead but he heard his two brothers Leon and Jakob survived. He became somewhat depressed since he lost seven members of his immediate family!

Finally, in 1947 he was reunited with his brothers. During that time he developed vague somatic symptoms such as headaches, weakness, and dizziness and was seen by a lot of private physicians. In 1948 he was sent to a TB sanitarium in the foothills of the Bavarian Alps in Germany. This is where he was treated for tuberculosis. This place was called Schloss-Elmau. My father shared with my mother that part of the treatment was to breath in the fresh air outside. The sanatorium was there until 1951 and was available for Displaced Persons. When he started feeling better he tried to immigrate to the US and by that time his tuberculosis was arrested and he was allowed to come to Detroit. Since his two brothers were not Holocaust survivors they were not allowed to enter the U.S. His brothers left for Australia. Unfortunately, my father and his brothers were once again separated for the rest of their lives!

In 1952 my father arrived in New York and then came to Detroit. He was a patient at the North End Clinic where his TB was inactive. He continued to have a number of somatic symptoms such as headaches almost daily and dizziness. He also suffered from nervousness. He had a number of fears, startle reactions, and anxiety which were all a result of the war. He suffered from tinnitus and vertigo in the left ear as well as a permanent sensorineural hearing loss after being hit and beaten.

It is so painful to hear that my father suffered from chronic problems related to the somatization of his anxiety. He turned his aggression against himself and somatized it; which is characteristic of the way that most victims of the Holocaust had to handle their problems because there was absolutely no outlet for their aggression except to turn it against themselves.

He was troubled with a great deal of survivor's guilt, especially because his younger brothers, two older brothers, his sister and parents perished in the concentration camps. The other two older brothers, Jakob and Leon survived since they were in Russia.

Dr. Heny Krystal, MD, was a psychiatrist, Holocaust trauma expert and survivor practicing in Michigan. It was suggested that my parents go to him for help. Dr. Krystal helped my father deal with his survivor's guilt. He also stated that my father felt his "parents disappeared somewhere," when in fact the majority of elderly people perished in Auschwitz. The doctor felt this was my father's way of denial that is involved in his avoidance of the fact that they were murdered. It's his avoidance of confronting himself with his survivor guilt, which is at the bottom of his anxiety, namely that he was fearful because he was afraid that he would be punished for surviving the war that his parents suffered in death. As a result of this, he had a variety of problems, all of which can be directly traced to the Nazi persecution. Prior to his persecution, he did not have any evidence of a predisposition to emotional or physical ailments.

I was unsure whether or not I should share this personal information in this book. On the one hand my father never shared it with anyone besides his doctors. When I told my daughter, Michelle, about my conundrum she stated that "It could have been that it was difficult for him to talk about it, not necessarily that he didn't want us to know." She has a valid point. We have had the utmost respect for my father and loved him unconditionally. This suffering made him a different person than whom he would have been without the war, but we loved him just the way he was. And so once again I will say the words he told me over and over again, "Ikh hab dir lib" which means "I love you" in Yiddish.

"For evil to flourish, it only requires good men to do nothing."
—Simon Wiesenthal

"He who passively accepts evil is as much involved in it as he who helps to perpetrate it. He who accepts evil without protesting against it is really cooperating with it."
—Dr. Martin Luther King Jr.

Chapter 7 The Parallel Lives Between Two Pairs Of Sisters
(Sophie Klisman and her sister Felicia Shloss to Dr. Edith Eva Eger and her sister Magda)

As I read Dr. Eger's book *The Choice: Embrace the Possible*, I was reflecting upon how similar the relationships were between my mom and aunt and Dr. Eger and her sister. Since all four of them were in several concentration camps in the Holocaust there was so much pain and suffering in their lives. Dr. Eger stated just because someone suffers does not mean they have to consider themselves a victim. One can choose to move forward. They were all victims of crime but that does not have to define who they are. Don't let the horrific past define who you are. Know that you can still have a fulfilling life and move forward.

Aunt Felicia had many wonderful events happen in her life after the war, such as two beautiful daughters and having her daughters get married. She became a grandmother and great grandmother. There were many simchas in her life.

When I reflect on my mother, I believe she tried not to portray herself as a victim. Was it because she was younger and had more attention as a child, due to the large age gap between her and her siblings? We may never know. All I know is she did not share or discuss her tragic life with me or my brother. She stated she did not want us to feel sorry for her, think less of her, or pity her. She wanted us to grow up as normal, healthy children with a lot of love. I can honestly say Mark and I had an amazing childhood with love, support, approval, affection, and lots of attention. She mastered the ability to make us feel whole. We felt no different than any other child born in the USA. We had the luxury of having our college paid for and more! We were not spoiled but rather appreciated how hard our parents worked and the sacrifices they made to make sure we were comfortable.

Both pairs of sisters were treated inhumanely. All of them were shoved in cattle cars meant for cattle, not for humans. Did they know the inhumanity was just starting? Finally the doors opened and there was the notorious sign "Arbeit Macht Frei." Work sets you free. As my mother stated, the chaos began. German shepherds were barking, people were screaming, people were being pushed around by armed SS soldiers, and people were being separated from their family members. Dr. Eger and my mother both shared the same scenarios. Nobody was explaining anything to the new arrivals. It was pure chaos. Soldiers were shouting which direction people

4,456 Miles

Sophie Klisman (Zysla Tajch)
from Living Witnesses Faces of the Holocaust *by Monnie Must.*

Felicia Shloss (Fajga Tajch)

needed to go to. Others were screaming. Men were forced into one line while the other line had women and children. Everyone inched forward not knowing where they were going or what would happen next. Dr. Eger and her sister went through the selection with Dr. Mengele and were sent to the right.

My mother was stopped by presumably Dr. Mengele, the notorious angel of death. He shouted "STOP" and asked her age and then he wanted to know her birthdate. My mother was petrified at that moment because he singled her out. She thought she did something wrong and was going to be shot at that instant. Somehow she had the courage to lie in order to be older. She had an intuition at that moment that it was better to be older. This allowed her to be with her sister. They hugged each other and cried. At that time they did not know if going to the right line meant life or death but they were thrilled they were together.

The elderly, sick and very young were sent to the showers and then the crematorium. These were no ordinary showers. Instead of water coming out of the showers poisonous fumes were released. The crematorium was burning bodies and ashes were being spit out of the chimney. There was a horrible stench as well.

Dr. Eger lost her parents in the crematorium while my mother lost her parents in the ghetto. Although drastically different deaths, they were both so horribly painful. My mother and her sister had memories of their own beautiful and loving parents and siblings. Now it was just the two of them, Fajga and Zysla.

The sisters each had to find a way to survive day by day. One can only wonder how my mother and aunt survived each and every day when death was so rampant everywhere. Was it because they had each other? Was it because they lived by their mantra of hope. Both my mother and aunt looked out for each other. My aunt shared her bread with my mother and helped my mother when she was sick. Mom looked out for her as well. My aunt was ten years older than my mother, so she took on the motherly role. They both transcended their own needs and committed to each other.

Even with shaven heads they still had their internal beauty. They were still beautiful people regardless of the external changes. First I thought the Nazis shaved their hair to make them feel less beautiful and less human. While in Poland I heard the purpose of this cruel act was to use the hair to stuff pillows, line boots for warmth, etc. All the sisters must have at some point felt anger, grief and fear. As Dr. Eger put it, you can hold on to those feelings or try to release them. It takes a strong person not to hold on to that bitterness. I wonder how many people were able to do that without therapy. I view my mother as a hero and someone who was able to let go of this anger, grief, and fear after the war. She stated it was because she started her own family and had to move on.

All the sisters must have somehow discovered an inner strength, even though the outside world became so intense and horrific. The sisters had to live day by day, hour by hour and minute by minute to survive. This may have been the way they kept themselves alive. I wonder how many people were able to do this. One has to have such a remarkable mindset to have that power.

Mom said she eventually heard explosions. Aunt Felicia said "Hang on a little while longer. I have a feeling the war is going to end soon." Mom would say the Germans would not bomb themselves. This is where the hope came in. The end was almost near.

As time progressed my mother became very sick and could not get up for roll call. Another time my mother had a horrible sore throat and felt it was strep throat. At times she just didn't have the strength to go on and just wanted to die. To tell an SS guard you did not feel well would mean death. There were no medications. Fortunately there was an inmate who was a nurse and she said there is no water or salt to gargle with and no medicine here in the camps. You will have to gargle with your urine. This is what she did and she feels this saved her life. Miraculously they survived!

My mother and her sister were liberated by the US Army on April 14, 1945. They could not imagine what freedom would look like. She thought she would yell, celebrate and then have a normal life. Mom was so weak and could barely stay awake. Some survivors died after being liberated by eating themselves to their death. They had to gradually stretch their stomach. Many survivors had lice, typhus and other horrible illnesses. The fear set in on where to live and how to survive. Were there any other survivors?

Anti-semitism was still rampant after the war. My mother and aunt had to recover in the Displaced Persons camps. They decided not to go back to their home in Lodz for fear of the Poles killing them. They heard stories of people being killed when they went back to their homes or when they would look for their buried treasures in the yard.

It took four long years for my mother and her sister to finally get their immigration papers. My mother and her sister were fortunate to finally leave Germany, with the new members of their family, Felicia's husband Roman and their daughter Loretta. Sophie was assigned to a different boat from the one Felicia, Roman and Loretta traveled in, but they all met in New York on June 18, 1949. Eventually they made their way to Michigan. With no family in Michigan, they had help from the Red Cross and the Jewish Agencies to find a little place to live in Detroit, Michigan.

My father and his brothers unfortunately were separated again after the war. My father Bernard and his two older brothers ended up in different countries. My dad came to the US while his brothers ended up in Melbourne, Australia. Bernie came alone by boat to the US in December 22, 1949. Eventually he also made his way to Michigan.

Uncle Israel Tajch, their father's brother left Poland before the war to go to Uruguay but because of the distance they were not reunited with him. Eventually they would meet but not for several years.

Once in the USA my mother had a desire to go back to school but the Red Cross said there are no funds for that. She had to get a job during the day and go to night school. Mom, who did not know English, had to work in a laundromat but she said she was grateful to work and earn some money. She learned English. My mother shared the story of wanting to learn English after the war in Germany. She attempted to go to school there but was made fun of. She had to go back to second grade and was much taller than the other students since she was obviously much older than them. She did not know the German language so she was made fun of. She eventually dropped out. She did have a private tutor that came to help her learn English through songs.

She had to find a purpose to get up in the morning. My mother and aunt were slowly finding that purpose. That purpose was to get an education, get a family and make a new life. Whomever she marries won't know her parents or siblings. There will be no grandparents for her children.

Aunt Felicia took on the role of being Mom's mother. She was caring yet overprotective. Felicia told Uncle Roman to go watch Sophie as she went on a date. Felicia told Mom whom she liked and what she did not like about Mom's dates.

They survived because they had each other for protection and they had to live for each other. They were co-dependent on each other. My mother asked "Why did I survive while others stronger and older than me did not?" There was a lot of guilt for surviving while their parents and siblings all perished.

Many people tried to live as if their years in the Holocaust never existed. Would this be healthy though? This appeared to be a way of coping for many survivors. My parents did this as well. Get married,

4,456 Miles

I found this photo of the spot where my mother Sophie was in June 7, 1949 while she was waiting to immigrate to New York from Bremerhaven Port, Germany. Her boat left from that area.

have children and work. Don't discuss the tragedy. Many families believed the more they bury the past, the happier they will be. The survivors wanted a new beginning: a safe and fulfilling new start on life. No one discussed their past, not even with the other spouse. In my family there was no mention of it to anyone until Anne mentioned there was a school project and her son had to interview a survivor. Otherwise, this was a taboo topic. As my mother shared bits and pieces of her story, she did not want us to be sad or affected by her past.

Therapists would say one needs to talk about his/her experiences, scream and cry, get therapy, etc. in order to heal. Stress was extremely common. Oftentimes people think of this (in a Diagnostic Statistic Manual) as a disorder when in reality it is a normal response when one suffers a trauma. Being Holocaust survivors is about the biggest trauma I can ever envision, especially since the trauma lasted for years and years. One instance of stress that I can recall was from many years ago with my father in the car. He was driving and a police turned on his siren. My father was stopped for speeding. As the police officer approached our vehicle my father broke down in tears and was trembling. I thought this was a strong reaction my father had when he was asked to show his license and registration.

Then I realized it was due to stress. This was a flashback from the SS soldiers from the concentration camps he was in. The pain and suffering was still fresh even though he was in a safe country. Now I realized this was a normal response due to the trauma in his life. I wish I had the insight at that moment. Well at least he got out of the speeding ticket. How many stress episodes did they experience? Situations that may appear minor to you and I could cause severe reactions within others.

Even though he was in a safe country the trauma remains internally. When does it subside, if ever. His panic may have always been within him. He along with my mother hid their pain and suffering from their children. The more one hid their fears the worse it becomes.

Not until 2015 did Mom speak about the Holocaust. She probably wore a mask, and pretended this horrific period in her life did not exist. When working at Casual Corner, she tried to make sure no one knew she was born in Poland. She was fortunate not to have a heavy dialect like so many survivors had. She camouflaged herself with all her coworkers. Not a word was spoken about the Holocaust during her and my father's professional careers. With encouragement from Anne my mother became a speaker at the Holocaust Memorial Center. Anne became a fabulous docent for the Center, and Mom was an exceptional speaker. Both Anne and my mother made this deal a reality. And so my mother's dream of becoming a teacher finally came to fruition. She is educating students and adults about the atrocities of the Holocaust at the Holocaust Memorial Center in Farmington Hills, Michigan.

By teaching others she is healing herself. Also, by going back to Poland in 2016 with her family and retracing her past, putting up a tombstone for her family and outwardly grieving, it helped her to heal. I learned healing is a tentative state. One day you may feel healed while another day you may not. Being able to go back to Auschwitz-Birkenau Concentration and Extermination Camp and leave on her own terms showed she defeated Hitler. She also spoke about her life at the synagogue in Piotrkow, Poland; the place where she attended as a child. She displayed strength, courage and power in educating other Jewish young professionals from New York, J.Roots. Whether she realizes it or not she is healing and getting some closure!

It took over 70 years and 4,456 miles back to Poland to get some closure. She is one of the strongest survivors I know! She is admired and loved by all that know her. Not until many years later did Mom come to the realization that maybe she survived the war because she had her sister with her. The sisters were dependent on each other. The irony of the whole situation was in the Holocaust my mother and aunt got along because they only had each other to depend on for survival. After the war there were more issues that arose, such as sharing others in their lives and not being the center of each other's life. My aunt had to share my mom with my father, and my parent's friends. Although Felicia was still receiving love from mom, it was different now. Perhaps my aunt had control of one thing in the war and that was taking care of my mom.

Now that the war was over she no longer had that same control. Mom needed freedom to live her life. This is where conflicts arose. During the war my aunt, being the older sister took on the mother role. By being older and her having to take on more responsibility she may have worried more. This may have contributed to her having more stress. Once again, this is a normal response to what she and the other survivors endured. Although raised in the same household, Aunt Felicia experienced some harder times than my mother did. Felicia remembered being homeless as a child and she and her family moved into their grandparent's home. There were many financial challenges growing up in Piotrkow and Lodz. Liba and Icek Berek Tajch moved their family in with Icek Berek's parents. This was before my mother, Zysla/Sophie was born. Conditions were extremely difficult and bleak. Another painful situation was in 1926, one of Icek Berek's and Liba's daughter Esteria passed away at the age of 9. My mother just heard stories about her, since my mother was not born yet. This was a devastating loss for the whole family and of course for my Aunt Felicia, since Esteria was her older sister.

At the age of 41, Liba and Icek Berek Tajch had another daughter, Zysla Tajch/ Sophie Klisman. My mother talked about all the love she felt growing up. She received a lot of attention from her parents even in tough times. My mother stated she never felt poor or deprived of anything. She had fond memories of taking walks in the park with her mom and getting fresh air. Her parents showed lots of love and affection to all kids but since the other children were older they may have had more time with Zysla.

Fajga and Zysla must have had a big bond in Piotrkow and Lodz being the only two sisters. The bond continued in the war. They found hope and strength within themselves.

I wonder how many survivors felt guilty for surviving the war while other family members were killed. One had to create a purpose to make them feel worthy of starting a new life. My mother started with her education. She pursued night school and I remember her taking lessons on TV in order to get her high school equivalency. My aunt raised Loretta and then had another daughter, Marla. Her purpose in life was to protect their children and shield them from harm. The survivors wanted to make sure their children never experienced hardship, prejudice or anti-Semitism. This was a new beginning. Being a mother and also working as a seamstress was the beginning for Felicia.

In America my mother silenced her past. Eventually Dr. Eger and Mom discovered that telling their story can help with the healing process. They had a choice to bury the past or teach others about the past. Dr. Eger, Mom, and Aunt Felicia all found the strength to talk about the past. Felicia did it right away while Mom and Dr. Eger did it later on in life. They all suffered greatly and talking about their past did not alleviate their suffering but it gave them the satisfaction of educating others.

Suffering happens to everyone but not to this extent. No one can escape some disappointment, health issues, financial burdens, etc. This kind of suffering (being put in prisons, being tortured, being starved to death) is beyond inhumane. Some people respond to suffering by being a vigilante and punish those that caused their suffering. Unfortunately in the camps one cannot be a vigilante. Others somehow tried to move forward. Holding on to the anger does not help people heal. The past does not have to determine how you will live in the present. The past has to be put in the past as no one from the Holocaust had any control of their life. What they do have control of is the present and their future.

Some survivors continued to be victims even after the war. They had a hard time moving forward. Other survivors somehow thrived through simchas from their children and grandchildren, finding success in their careers, going on to get education, meeting other survivors and making them their new family, etc. My parents miraculously choice to move forward and to live lives they were proud of.

My mother and aunt had hope. Without hope it would be a devastating world. Never give up on hope! Even today, no matter what the situation is, my mother still preaches have hope!

And now Mom is speaking so future generations don't have to relive the past. Mom is making the world a better place to live by helping to eradicate prejudice and anti-Semitism. She is teaching all nationalities about hatred and bigotry. Her parents would have been so proud of how Aunt Felicia and Mom rose above this hatred and worked to make this world a better place to live. By finally going back to Poland and placing a tombstone in honor of their family and placing pebbles on the tombstone, they honored their parent's and sibling's lives. The pebble lets others know the dead will always be alive in our hearts and memories. We will never, ever forget them.

The journey to Poland was one of the most difficult yet meaningful trips of my life. One day, I hope my children will go to Poland and help keep that memory alive!

Lori Klisman Ellis

Lodz ghetto children in line to be deported to death camps, Sept. 1942
(wikimedia public domain photo)

Chapter 8 Summary Of Oral Testimony On Sophie Klisman & Felicia Shloss

Let me start with what makes Sophie Tajch Klisman and Felicia Tajch Shloss such extraordinary women? Is it because they survived being in the ghetto for five years and survived three concentration camps; which gave them inner strength? Is it because they rarely gave up hope? Is it because they were so strong to survive starvation, the cold, brutality and the loss of their family? Or is it because they grew up in a loving household and that gave them the foundation needed to survive the worst hardships in the world? Is it because they were lucky, had hope, had each other, had determination and courage? Who knows but one thing is for sure we were blessed to have the two of them survive!

Here is Sophie's story:
This information was taken from her interview from Zieva Konvisser on June 24, 2013.

Sophie was the youngest of four siblings in Lodz. She had a happy childhood, loved and cared for. In 1939, World War II broke out and her whole life turned into chaos. She was only 10 years old and she remembers bombing, schools shutting down for the Jewish people, being forced to evacuate her home and told to move to the ghetto. As if this was not bad enough, she was forced to work in a knitting shop for 12 hours a day with limited rations of food. She had to experience starvation and witness her beloved parents and older brother, Moszek (Moniek), die before her very eyes.

Her mother asked for a piece of bread. They were allotted one piece of bread for the day. She gave her food to her children. Now I understand when there is a hard end piece of bread in the loaf and I used to want to toss it out, Mom would say "I want that piece for my sandwich. I like that piece." She had sensitive teeth so I never understood why she wanted it. Now one can understand that a piece of bread could make the difference between life and death. Her mother's generosity and bravery saved my mother and aunt.

Sophie stated there were no funerals but merely a wagon came by and bodies were piled up in there. She never knew what happened to them. She feared she would be next. To have found my grandmother's burial site in the Lodz ghetto was truly unbelievable to me and Mom. Who knew at the time some of the prisoners had to bury the dead? Lucky for us, the Germans were known to be meticulous at record keeping. So to have found her exact spot and Moniek's exact spot was a blessing!

Somehow my mother, Felicia, and Israel went on working, starving, and mourning their family. Every few weeks Nazi soldiers would invade their dwelling looking for males. Israel/Srulek hid when he heard the Nazis barging in the door. How frightening for young kids to have to stand up to Nazis.

The ghetto liquidated in 1944. The three survivors of the Tajch family were sent into box cars not knowing where to go. My mother stated this was one of the most frightening things she experienced. To be locked in a box car with no windows, no air circulating, no lights, no toilets, and crammed with people and not knowing whether you were going to survive or die was surreal.

When the box cars opened she saw the sign "Auschwitz." Now the chaos began. Dogs barking, armed soldiers, big German Shephard dogs barking, people screaming and crying. Anybody that made a noise was hit over the head. They were sent for the showers and they thought these were the gas showers. Luckily they malfunctioned and water came out. They were shaved and disrobed. They went through the selection. She miraculously survived with her sister. She cried as her brother was sent with the males. He looked back and cried. They waved goodbye. How heart wrenching to not know if they would ever see each other again. That was the very last time she and her sister saw him.

Sophie talked in length about the selection process. She lied about her age, stating she was 18 instead of 15. She said she was born in 1926 instead of 1929. To be able to calculate this in the face of death was truly remarkable. After working in camp, having roll calls three times a day and suffering they were again put in box cars and sent to Bergen-Belsen. Once again, she wondered where she and her sister would be going. Would they survive? Could conditions be just as horrific?

These barracks were different than those at Auschwitz. In Bergen-Belsen there was not pieces of wood to be used as bunk beds. Now they had to sleep on the ground, with a little hay. It seems unimaginable to sleep on the ground in the cold and in the rain without a pillow or blanket. This is where my mother became very sick. To have strep throat with no medicine, be cold and not have food or medical care, was almost not worth the fight. My mother was willing to give up at that point. Felicia told her "Don't leave me. You can't die. You're so young, were going to fight it. We're going to survive." Even without medicine, she survived somehow.

My mother shared that there was a Holocaust survivor who used to be a nurse. She encouraged Mom to gargle however there was no water. She told her to gargle with her urine. No matter how horrible it was, my mother felt that helped her survive.

Once again she was put in box cars and they were sent to Salzwedel Concentration camp. She worked from six at night to six in the morning. They had to walk a couple of miles in the snow to get there. She talks about not having any warm clothes or shoes. I can't help but think about when it is below freezing in Michigan and having a warm sweater, heavy boots, and a thick coat, hat, and mittens that I still complain. How would I have survived? I think I would not have made it. As my mother said, it was easier to die than to survive.

At this time, November 1944 they started hearing bombs go off. They were hopeful the war was coming to an end. She had to hold on. The miracle happened on April 14, 1945. The prisoners were liberated. She said "As long as I live to be 100, I will never forget that date." Her testimony continues about the challenges of moving forward after liberation. Her full oral history will be included in the addendum called the "Ellis/Klisman Family Tree."

Here is Felicia's story:

Felicia recalls a loving family. She had traditional Friday night dinners and some Jewish soldiers were guests at their residence. She was born in Piotrkow and at 13 or 14 she along with her family moved to Lodz, Poland. Her mother's family (Aunt) lived in Paris, France. Her father would sometimes help his grandfather print books and newspapers at Cedarbaum's Print shop. They worked on Jewish books. Felicia stated she went to the theater before the war broke out.

Felicia remembers the day the Germans arrived in Lodz, Poland with large tanks. It was a frightening experience. She said Poland did not have these huge tanks. The German soldiers took all the equipment from the factories the Jews owned. Life was quickly changing for the worse in Poland. They were no longer allowed to stand in line at the grocery store to purchase bread. The Jews were beaten by the Polish police. They had curfews and eventually were not allowed to go out. She remembers the Germans killing her aunt. She spoke about her aunt owning a bakery store. This was an aunt on her father's side.

Conditions were getting so bad and they were eventually forced to relocate to the Lodz ghetto. There was no heat there and they had to barter for food. Felicia recalls taking some of her mother's silverware and bartering for food for the family. She was worried that her mother would be mad at her for taking this.

Felicia stated there were at least 200 deaths a day due to starvation and cold conditions. She recalls the death of her brother in the ghetto. She never mentioned the death of her parents in the ghetto. She may have been living in a different area than her family for a short time.

In the ghetto she was forced to make storm coats for the German soldiers and then became part of the kitchen help. She tried to steal food to bring home for her siblings. That seemed like the ideal job to be around food. She recalls her sister Zysla making tablecloths for export. Felicia recalls the people in charge: Chaim Rumkowski and Arthur Greiser.

She stated the sick were taken out of the ghetto, which meant they were killed. This left room for stronger people from other towns to join the people in the Lodz ghetto. Felicia mentioned she was sent to a prison in August, 1944 for a few days prior to going on the box cars to Auschwitz.

Felicia recalls taking her possessions with her on the cattle car which included family pictures, some clothes, make up and a purse. Once she arrived in Auschwitz she was forced to leave all of her possessions for the Nazis to take. It must have been devastating to lose her family photos.

Upon entering the concentration camp she had to wear badges on her clothes signifying that she was Jewish. She recalls being put in block #26 where fifteen girls were in one bunk. She was provided a flimsy lightweight dress to wear. Some of the other inmates in other blocks that had been there for a while were wearing the striped uniforms. Conditions were overcrowded, unsanitary and the goal was to starve the prisoners. There were counts or roll calls at 4:00 a.m. This caused extreme exhaustion. She recalls eventually being transported to Bergen-Belsen and then Salzwedel. She was with her sister the whole time.

In Salzwedel the French workers did not wear uniforms and they would come to fix the ammunition machines, as they frequently malfunctioned. Some of the French men were sympathetic to the young woman and would on a rare occasion smuggle in potatoes and sandwiches for them. They would dump them in the garbage and told them to eventually look for them and eat them. (My mother stated on one rare occasion a German soldier must have been full and gave his sandwich to my mother.) When the German staff noticed the French men talking to the woman prisoners, the French men said they were explaining the machines to them rather than telling them about the hidden food. The German staff told the woman prisoners not to talk to the men.

Felicia recalls the Germans forcing them to have number plates and calling them "hunds" or dogs. They would take away their individual identity. One German approached Felicia in a rough way and said make sure you put the caps on the guns because the Greek Jews were stupid and did not know the German language. As a result of this, one girl did not follow directions and the ammunition machine backfired the bullet and hit her chest and neck. She died. So there was always the fear of getting killed by the equipment malfunctioning as well as getting hit and killed by the German guards or staff.

Felicia recalls my mother becoming very ill and one Jewish prisoner worked on the grounds in a hospital-like ward or room. My mother was taken there and given a green pill. My mother threw up the pill and could not keep anything down. At that time she was told she had damage to her liver. She stayed there approximately three days. Felicia helped to clean the room so my mother could stay there longer. Upon her discharge, her fellow inmates commented on how much my mother grew, from the extra sleep. Thank goodness she grew because today she stands at merely five feet two inches tall.

Felicia also recalls having one bunk bed which was made of a sack of straw for each person to lay on. Since the climate was so cold, my aunt and mother shared one bed and put the straw sack over them for a make shift blanket. This helped keep them a little bit warmer. There was also no warm water. There was cold running water so they would wash themselves with it. Felicia also washed a dress she had in cold water and hung it up overnight to dry.

On liberation day there were loud explosions that were getting closer and closer. Some German soldiers were running away. Eventually a few American soldiers opened up the gates to liberate them. One person took revenge on a German soldier running and Felicia saw him getting killed. The Mayor allowed the soldiers to knock down store doors in Germany to get the prisoners food and clothes. Felicia brought back some food. She said she had a difficult time swallowing the food. My mother was still in the bunk sleeping. Felicia also brought back some clothes for herself, her sister and her brother, with the hopes of finding him. Tragically she never found him, so she eventually gave the clothes to another person.

She had the option of going back to Lodz, Poland with her sister but she heard the people in the town would kill Jewish children and did not want to go back. She recalled her brother saying to her, keep in touch with our uncle in South America. So she wanted to go there. Felicia also shared she had hopes of finding her parents and brother upon liberation. She must have been in a different location in the ghetto for a while, for her not to have seen them perish in the ghetto as my mother witnessed. Or maybe it was survivor's guilt to not want to think about them dying. Felicia talked about her dreams in the camps. She dreamt she saw her parents and brother frequently. She also said she heard her father give her messages on how to stay alive.

After the war Felicia married Roman and had children. She stated how much her children meant to her and how she loved them very much. She was so proud of their careers. She said one daughter was Loretta and was married and lived in Texas. Her other daughter was named Mary in order to hide her Jewish identity. However when Mary was sixteen and applied for her driver's license, she decided to formally change her name to Marla. Marla also got married.

Felicia went back to school and learned how to design clothes. She took pride in making her own clothes for her daughters and for herself. She made me a birthday dress at a young age. I recall her making a beautiful purple blazer that she wore for her grandson Sam's Bar Mitzvah. She worked at Hudson's store and was a seamstress there. Uncle Roman was a furrier. Together they worked hard to raise their two beautiful and educated daughters. Life was not always easy in the US but they tried hard.

My mother's family and my aunt's family both lived in the same city, Oak Park. We celebrated holidays together. There was a lot of love between the two sisters even though they were quite different people. My mother and my aunt dealt with the past differently—no one walked away without struggles, but there was a lot of love in our families.

Felicia Shloss' video recording by Dr. Sidney Bokovsky from University of Michigan, Dearborn in Feb., 1983 can be viewed at: http://holocaust.umd.umich.edu/interview.php?D=schloss *(Please note in this interview her last name was spelled Schloss.).* I have also included the written portion of Felicia's interview in the second part of this book: "Ellis/Klisman Family Tree."

Part III: Liberation/Post WWII

Chapter 9 Liberation April 14, 1945

Finally, her dreams of being liberated were answered. Years of hoping and praying came true. My mother and Felicia were liberated from Salzwedel in Germany by members of the 84th Infantry, Ninth U.S. Army on April 14, 1945! People always imagined they would scream and shout with elation, during this time and this may have been the case for many; however other prisoners like my mother felt too weak to even celebrate. Liberation day allowed her to go to sleep and only be woken by her sister, who provided her with food. Felicia ran out to get food with some other women. Additional information is provided in this book by her liberators.

On January, 2018 Lori Ellis contacted Salzwedel Museum to see if any documents or photos were still available on Zysla and Fajga Tajch. They did not have photos of the two of them, but they did have some records. The records did not reveal any additional information but I was amazed that there was some documentation.

After being liberated from Salzwedel, they went to their first Displaced Persons camp. Documentation from the 84th Infantry Division stated the women were transferred from their original camp to a modern home which happened to be Adolf Hitler's Barracks. General Bolling changed the name to Camp Vassar. In the meantime, the old camp at Salzwedel was burned down.

They had to learn how to eat food again and be nursed back to health with the help of medical staff and dieticians. Although free, there were many physical and emotional issues to deal with.

The women felt safe at the new camp. My mother and aunt were too frightened to return to Poland. They were told it was not safe to go back. Anti-Semitism was still rampant. Who from their family would still be alive? What are they going to do with their lives now? How will they pick up the pieces of their lost years? It was a frightening time for them. They were desperate to find answers on what happened to their brother, Israel. Tragically, they witnessed the death of their parents and Moszek in the ghetto, so now their only hope was finding Israel and possibly aunts and uncles.

Photos on next page: These three photos were taken on liberation day of the woman in Salzwedel in 1945. These photos were sent directly from the Neuengamme Archives from Hamburg, Germany to Lori Klisman Ellis.

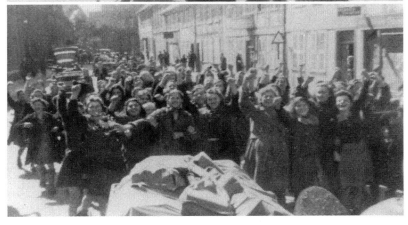

4,456 Miles

Chapter 10 After The Concentration Camps & Into The Displaced Persons Camps

"Whoever saves one life saves the entire world."
—Itzhak Stern

"Just as man cannot live without dreams, he cannot live without hope. If dreams reflect the past, hope summons the future."
—Elie Wiesel

THE miserable camp in Salzwedel was burned down and the women were transferred to the excellent Adolf Hitler Barracks which had housed the personnel of a Luftwaffe field. For the first time in years, they ate like human beings. The band played for them. In return, the women handed out drinks and flowers.

Camp Vassar (http://usgerrelations.traces.org/salzwedel.html)

59

After the liberation Sophie and Felicia were in Ainring Displaced Person (DP) camp. Ainring, Germany was near the border of Austria. During the war Ainring was a concentration camp but once those imprisoned were liberated they made these barracks into more comfortable quarters. They had their own beds, food, and medical care and so on. Unfortunately, there was a fire in Ainring and one of the barracks burned down. Luckily it was not their barrack.

During my mother's stay in Ainring there was a male survivor who was around 30 years old. He wanted to start a traveling theater. He selected my mother to be the main star. She was cast as a bride, wearing a white flower in her hair. The play was called "Mayn Vays Blyen" which means "My White Bloom." In the play her fiancé got killed in a fire. She learned to speak Yiddish in this play. The actors in the play traveled to various DP camps to perform. Felicia came to watch her performance and told my mother she was very nervous for my mother's opening debut. Obviously my mother enjoyed performing and was very good at it because she was asked to perform in another play. This occurred in 1946 or 1947.

Roman Shloss (Rachmiel Szlosbajtel) was also in Ainring and that is where my Aunt Felicia, (Fajga Tajch) met him. He was a very handsome young man, who was the sole survivor of his immediate family. Fortunately he had a cousin who survived. Roman wanted to go see his cousin in Regensburg, which is a city in southeast Germany. It is the fourth largest city in the state of Bavaria. His visit lasted approximately 5 weeks. Roman's cousin lived with an older woman in a private home there. Felicia and Roman started dating before he left to visit his cousin. Eventually my mother, Sophie and Felicia and Roman all moved to Regensburg which was a bigger city and had better conditions. Then they all moved to Bad Reichenhall Displaced Person's camp. This DP camp was in the mountains in Bavaria, Germany. My mother said it looked a bit like Frankenmuth, Michigan.

My mother remembers that she was in several different DP camps. In Ainring she met her first boyfriend, an older man named Yonik (John) Friedman. She was 16 and he was 25. He was from Czestochowa, Poland and was also a survivor. He eventually moved to South America. There was another young man, Simon, who was a survivor in the same DP camp. He liked my mother. My mother did not return his feelings though. He moved to Uruguay to be with his brother. It seemed that South America was a common place that many survivors went to. He was in touch with my mother's Uncle

4,456 Miles

Bad Reichenhall (wikimedia)

Israel and his family. Simon eventually got married there. Some time around 2008, Simon came to New York and called my mother. He wanted to see her and wondered how far it was from New York to Michigan. When he called her he said he was her boyfriend and called her by Zosia or Zysla. They did not meet up.

When Uncle Israel's wife died, he decided to come to Michigan and visit with my mother and my aunt. He was approximately 65–70 years old when he came for his visit. My mother said he did not know English but managed to make it to check in with his nieces. It took a lot of courage as well as a lot of money to travel alone internationally. He stayed with my aunt and then my mother for part of his visit. He talked about trying to sponsor his nieces right after the war and send them to Uruguay, but that never happened. My mother thought it was because the family grew: My aunt got married and had Loretta. Therefore, he would have had to sponsor four people and not two.

My mother, Aunt Felicia and Roman eventually relocated to Lampertheim DP camp. Lampertheim is a small town on the Rhine bank in Frankfurt. It was a DP camp at the end of 1945 all the way up to May, 1949. It was hard to believe that my mother and her sister were in D.P camps in Germany for four long years waiting to come to America. There were 1,200 Jewish displaced persons living there mainly from Poland. This DP camp was a more luxurious one as compared to the other ones.

There were private houses in the village. There were police and fire fighters in this village. There was also a post office which was operated as a tracing center for missing family members. There were doctors there as well, which were actually many displaced people themselves. It became an Orthodox community with one house transformed into a synagogue. They had a kosher kitchen for 90 DP's. There was an orchestra, a secular elementary school and a kindergarten. There were summer camps for children. Also there was a kibbutz to help people learn about farming. In addition there were courses offered in dressmaking and more.

While at Lampertheim, Sophie was doing office work and was trained to be a telephone operator. She worked in a sound proof room. She answered phones and connected people to whom they called. She learned how to use the telephone operator board or the switchboard operations. Sophie had to follow telephone etiquette such as speak clearly, be polite and courteous, and had to have good listening skills. She did not receive a pay check for her work but rather received a candy bar or peaches. Those goodies must have been a treat since during her time in the war there was nothing besides bread and watered down soup. During her time at this DP camp and others, many young gentleman had an interest in my mother. Since my mother is very modest, she requested that I do not share those stories about Lampertheim with others. We did chuckle about it though! I would say to Mom, when I was young I never realized that you and dad looked like movie stars. They were an extremely attractive couple.

Lampertheim (www.alemannia-judaica.de/lampertheim_synagoge.htm)

Chapter 11 Life After The War

*"Hatred Eats the Soul of the Hater,
Not the Hated."*
—Alice Herz Sommer

Sophie, Felicia, Roman and their daughter, Loretta left Germany in June, 1949 by boat to come to New York and they were elated to see the statue of liberty. While on a trip to Israel, Jeff and I saw a ship from the Haifa Naval Museum that was used to transport prisoners that were liberated out of concentration camps in Germany to Israel. As my mother stated it was not a cruise ship but it allowed people to come to a country that had freedom.

My mother and aunt, uncle, cousin and father were all slated to come to Detroit. The Jewish Family Service and Red Cross helped them immensely. My mother asked to go to school full time but the staff said "We are not able to pay for it. Work and go to night school." That is indeed what she did. She enrolled at Central High for night school in Detroit, Michigan. She worked in a Laundromat during the day. This is where she interacted with other Holocaust survivors and met her future husband, Bernard.

It took Bernard a while to start talking to Sophie as he was reserved. She couldn't help but notice that he was handsome and very neat. He was a very kind man. It took some time before they started dating. He asked her out however he did not have a car, so they walked to an ice cream parlor. They enjoyed each other's company. They lived in the Jewish section of Detroit, near Linwood Street. They had a lot in common. Although Bernard never spoke about his

past they both survived the camps and lost several family members. Bernard came to Detroit on December 22, 1949 which was his birthday. Sophie came to Detroit 6 months earlier, in June of 1949.

Other men asked her out but they were not as kind and good looking as Bernard. They dated for a while. Bernard wanted to get married although he was afraid to make the commitment because he did not have a lot of money saved up. Sophie said "Two people can live as cheap as one." She stated "I knew he loved me." Felicia also really liked him, probably because he was a quiet man. So they decide to get married the end of 1951. Sophie was only 22 years old. "There was not an official proposal of getting down on one knee, nor an engagement ring." Eventually Sophie received a ring. She stated she wore a beautiful white suit and went to the Rabbi's study in a synagogue to get married. Then they went to the court house to get the marriage license. Afterwards they went out to dinner with friends to celebrate.

December 10, 1951

There was not a honeymoon because they could not take time off from work. Eventually they took a train and went to a bed and breakfast resort in Canada. Mrs. Labelle, a large, old fashion woman from Lodz, Poland was the owner along with her younger husband. She was an excellent cook. There was not much to do there besides laying on the beach. They had a wonderful trip and had to head back home to go back to work.

Sophie and Bernard decided to save a lot of money prior to having children. They waited five years. They worked hard every day and saved every penny they could. They had a very conservative life style but were very happy. They felt very happy together and knew they had endless opportunities if they went to school, learned the language, and worked hard.

They were married 61 years. Sophie stated they had a wonderful marriage. They were loving, kind, respectful, helpful, and wonderful soulmates. They enjoyed spending time together, traveling, enjoying their children, and helping out with their children and grandchildren. They built a beautiful legacy together.

They lived in a tiny apartment on Pingree Street in Detroit when they were first married, then they moved to a small house on St. Mary Street. Mark was born and they lived on St. Mary Street until my mother was pregnant with Lori. Eventually they moved to 21660 Kipling in Oak Park, Michigan. After that they moved to 24783 Highland Drive in Novi, Michigan. This was a huge accomplishment to have their beautiful own homes. They were so proud to be homeowners.

Survivor friends soon became an integral part of my parents' lives. Without any family besides my one Aunt Felicia, her husband Uncle Roman, and their two children Loretta and Marla, there was no one else. My dad's two brothers Uncle Jakob and Uncle Leon lived on a different continent, in Australia. Soon the Weiss, Huppert, Kartush, Greenblatt, Tennenbaum, and Pilcowitz families were our extended family. I never felt unusual about having a small family until I met my

Rose & Ted Pilcowitz who survived the Holocaust

husband, Jeff. Soon I realized he had a huge family with several aunts, uncles, cousins and grandparents. When I was around his grandparents it was very emotional. I never had someone so elderly in my life. They lived in their upper 80's and some in their 90's. They were so lovely and kind. Then I began thinking about how unfair it was to not have grandparents. Even worse how tragic for my parents not to have parents! What a tragic life they had in the ghetto and the camps without parents.

Lori Klisman Ellis

Left to right: Sam and Giza Kartush, Martin and Sue Weiss, Sophie and Bernie Klisman and Moris and Rose Huppert at my daughter Michelle Ellis' Bat Mitzvah in 2001.

Photo Left: Leo Beals (Survivor) with Sophie Tajch Klisman
Photo Right: Moris Huppert (survivor), Sophie Klisman (Survivor) and Rebecca (Rita) Huppert Hupfrum (Born in a DP camp).

4,456 Miles

Then I thought about how fortunate my family was; we were small but loving. How did my parents manage without the support and guidance of their parents? My brother and I were so fortunate to have the support, guidance and love of our parents. What great, honest and law abiding people they were. How did they shield me from this evil? How did they not instill prejudice and hatred for the Germans and Poles? All I can think of was that, prior to the war, they must have had a lot of love in their lives, even though times were always tough in Poland. I can't imagine being poor to the point of starvation, having large families, and not having the modern conveniences of our life.

Their life during the war consisted of pure devastation. That was a living hell. The only wish is that people learn from past tragedies and never forget!

My mother always has a positive outlook on life. She would always say "Complaining does not help. Give compliments. Be genuine about the compliments you give. Compliments are free so why not give them out. It makes others feel good about themselves." That was a sure way to make friends and she has many friends. My mother also says she wants to be independent. She never wants to be a burden to others. She is all that and more! I am so lucky to have her in my life. I was so fortunate to have my kind and loving father in my life as well.

Lori Klisman Ellis

Chapter 12 From Tragedy To Triumph

"Remember the past to build on the future."
—Aish Minnesota, JCRC

Bernard Klisman in Michigan

Both of my parents had success in their careers. They got many accolades for their sales. When my father, Bernard first immigrated to the USA he did not know any English. He worked at Hudson Motor Company. He eventually learned the language and had more opportunities. He worked for Buster Brown and won a marvelous trip in 1962 to New York. He was also employed at Hanes, Hayman and Company, J. Krolick and Company, Wetsman and Company, and Levy and Company. He was a hard worker and very conscientious. He was extremely handsome as well.

My father loved fixing things around the house. He finished a basement in our home in Oak Park. He created a bar and many rooms in the basement. He enjoyed doing this type of work. He would come to my house and my brother's house and fix everything. He even put up wallpaper in the baby's room before my daughter was born. We really appreciated his talents. He would always say he is not a professional; but now I know why it looked so professional. His years in the camps doing manual labor and using various tools. He had to be a perfectionist; otherwise there were terrible consequences. That is why his work was always so perfect.

My mother was the top sales woman in her region at Casual Corner. She was a fashion consultant and a sales woman. She won many awards. Prior to that she worked at B. Siegel department store. She is so beautiful and stylish. She had an excellent eye for fashion. Her granddaughter, Michelle took after her in the fashion industry as well.

Both of my parents were obviously extremely hard workers. As my mother mentioned she was grateful to work hard, make money, buy a house, have a family and appreciated all of it. These are things many of us may take for granted but not them. Life was busy for them. They had integrated into a normal life.

They worked hard at putting the past horrific experiences behind them and moved forward. They provided us with little information about the Holocaust. It was not discussed until my niece and nephew did a book report on the Holocaust. My sister-in-law asked many questions as well.

Eventually my sister-in-law retired and my mother wanted her to be a docent at the Holocaust Memorial Center. My sister-in-law said she would only do it if my mother became a speaker about the Holocaust.

Sophie in the US c. 1950

Now they are a dynamic duo. They both take an active role volunteering at the Holocaust Memorial Center. They are making a huge impact on everyone who enters the Museum.

My mother once said she always wanted to become a teacher, but due to the war she was never able to do that. With the desire to further her education, she took night classes and continued taking courses when she was a young girl. Sophie became very proficient in English and did not have a dialect. She eventually acquired her GED. Now she is teaching others about the atrocities of the war. She is an outstanding teacher! We are proud of her accomplishments.

> *"Joy comes into our lives when we have something to do, someone to love and something to hope for."*
>
> —*Victor Frankl*

Part IV: Poland Here We Come 70 Plus Years Later

Chapter 13 How My Interest In Poland Began

My interest was piqued on the topic of genealogy when Ina, a colleague of mine, posted "The Memory Project" on Facebook. I went on that site and to my surprise I found the names of my family that I never had the opportunity to meet since they had perished in Poland during the Jewish ghetto and Holocaust. They are on the World Memory Project: Connecting Shoah Survivors with their roots. The website is www.ushmm.org/online/world-memory-project/.

I saw my ancestor's birth dates and death dates. I shared this information with my mother and she contacted a local synagogue, Adat Shalom, and her and Rabbi Bergman created plaques in memory of her beloved mother, father and two brothers. Now the family will have a place to go to cherish the memories of her family, since there were no tombstones or funerals for them. At that time, we thought this was a little closure.

A few weeks later I ran into an acquaintance of mine, Karen at the JCC who shared with me that there was a genealogy website

Our beautiful plaques at Adat Shalom, in Farmington Hills, Michigan.

called www.Jewishgen.org that has databases, resources and research tools to help those with Jewish ancestry. I thought this would be helpful to find more information on our family. And so the search began.

Lo and behold, I came across some valuable information. I found the exact location of my grandmother Liba and Uncle Moszek Tajch's burial site in the Lodz Cemetery in Poland. I started exploring other websites as well to make sure this information was accurate. I came across several other sites that confirmed this information.

I then went to the Holocaust Memorial Center in Farmington Hills, MI with my sister-in-law Anne and met with the librarian, Feiga Weiss, and she had many more valuable websites for me to search. I became so engrossed in my Jewish Heritage that I researched information daily. I began finding more and more valuable information on my family that I never knew. Anne and I contacted the Holocaust Memorial Center in Washington DC to see if they could track down any more information and family photos. My mother, Sophie and her sister, Felicia did not have any photos of their family. The Nazis' destroyed all their possessions including any family photos they had.

I knew if we could find a photo it would be like hitting the lottery. Well to my surprise a few days later I got a phone call from a staff member at the Holocaust Memorial Center that she

found a photo of my Uncle Moszek. She told me he was a handsome young boy. I waited weeks for this photo to come in the mail and when it did I began to cry. He resembled my brother, Mark and my nephew, Aaron. I could not wait to send it to my mother who was in Florida for the winter. Since she did not have her computer with her, I emailed the photo to her friend's cell phone and had Mom go over there to view it.

My mother was so anxious to see it. She had not seen her brother in 77 years. She stated she probably would not recognize him. As soon as she saw the photo she began to cry. She said she did recognize him and that was his school photo. He was so strikingly handsome and so young. The family immediately went to get copies of his photo and enlarge it. This was a treasure! We now have a beautiful photo of Moszek!

Next, we found a document from the Holocaust Center with an extremely dark photo of another brother, Israel. It was too dark to make out. We contacted Poland to find the original documents which would have been on Microfiche but had no luck. This was the brother that was last seen in Auschwitz. I tried contacting the Auschwitz Museum but staff replied many documents were destroyed prior to liquidation.

Next I searched all documents from Yad Vashem and came up with no photos. I did see documentation there that stated my mother and aunt perished in the Holocaust, so after 77 years, I sent in corrected documentation that they survived.

I searched documentation from the "Holocaust Survivors and Victims Database" and found documentation on each family member that had information on it such as the place of birth, their address, their occupation, the date of death, and more.

I was on a mission to find as much as I could. I searched the "Jewish Records Indexing—Poland" (JRI-Poland) that Stanley Diamond started and this confirmed once again the information on the exact burial spots of some of my family members: my grandmother Liba Tajch and my uncle Moszek Tajch. I also came

4,456 Miles

across many other Tajch names which were probably from our family, but my mother did not recognize their names. Each person had a death date, an age, a father's name, and the location of their burial. This was so hard to believe, as my mother said there was a massive amount of people dying daily from starvation, so how could they all have been buried. She said a wagon came and piled up the bodies and removed them. That was it. No funeral service, no prayers, no time for mourning. No closure! Well to my surprise, I found out the Germans were meticulous about keeping records, so they tagged their toes with their names. Who knew this would come in handy 77 years later?

Another site that I searched and had luck with was the "Central Data Base of Shoah Victims' Names." This site had all the family names and dates of birth, hometowns, places they were during the war, permanent places or residence, streets in the ghetto, place of death, date of death, and more. It also stated if they were murdered or if they were missing, then it stated "presumably murdered." I got confirmation that the family all lived on the same street in the Jewish ghetto in Lodz. This address was confirmed by my mother. Now we have an address in Lodz. I began wondering what would be there now. I decided to search the app Google Earth and see if there was anything that showed up in that spot. Sure enough, there was something still there!

Above is the New Lodz Cemetery in the Ghetto Fields prior to the tombstone. This is where Liba Rozrazowska Tajch and Moszek Tajch were buried. All that was needed was a beautiful tombstone and the family to go to Lodz to perform a service in memory of my mom's beautiful family. **(wikimedia)**

Lori Klisman Ellis

My sister-in-law Anne and I started filling out forms online to the "International Tracing Society" to continue the search that was done at least 50 years ago by my Aunt Felicia, to see if we could find her brother Israel. My mother and Aunt never saw or heard from him after they went through the selection process in Auschwitz Concentration Camp. Unfortunately they did not have any records to verify or deny that he was murdered.

Surprisingly we found out he was sent to Bergen-Belsen Concentration camp, the same one that my mother and Aunt were sent to. They never knew their brother was there as well. What happened to him there? I contacted the Bergen-Belsen Museum and there were no more records. One can only presume that he perished there.

I also googled "Children of the Lodz Ghetto" and to my surprise my mother's polish name popped up. There was a young student named Emily taking a college class on Judaism at a University in Washington D.C. Her Professor assigned them to do research on children of the Holocaust. She happened to select my mother, Sophie Klisman. Her name in Poland was Zysla Tajch. I read the information she had written and was amazed that her research was 100% accurate. She found out and documented her birth date, her ghetto street address, her parents and siblings names, and more. Her professor monitored her work and would guide her on her research. She stopped when she no longer had information on her after her stay in Auschwitz.

I kept rereading this information and desperately searching for the author. I checked Facebook, I tried to find her on Skype and then I found several young females with her name on Linkedin. I thought she would be thrilled to hear from me and my mother. Well finally at the end of her research I posted a comment, that if Emily happens to read this I wanted to let her know my mother Zysla is still alive and survived the camps. I also wanted to confirm that her research was 100% accurate. Well the next day I got an email from her stating that she could not believe she heard from us. She said she never imagined something like this could happen. Emily said she enjoyed doing this research and even after completing the class she continued to do work on it. Emily and I were thrilled to be able to chat online and connect!

From reading Emily's post I found out the name of my mother's school. It was School #9B and it was a school for girls in Lodz. The students attended classes in the afternoon. Most students were between 10 and 16 years of age and were born between 1925 and

4,456 Miles

1931. This school was located at Ulica Rybna 15. The street name was changed to Fischstrasse when German occupation began in 1939. In May 1942 a slippers department was located there.

I also went on Ancestry.com and started putting in names of a few family members that I knew. I would pick Mom's brain to see who her siblings were and if she recalled any aunts and uncles, grandparents, etc. Since she was so young, Mom could only recall her immediate family's names. She unfortunately could not recall many other names. Once I put in the few names that she knew and their birthdates, a leaf would appear on the tree—a hint of possible other family members. Later I found out this information was provided to Ancestry.com from JRI-Poland. It was helpful as it brought up names, birthdates, and more. I started learning who was in our family. Now I can share this information with my children and cousins. I was so excited.

I was told by some staff members at the Holocaust Memorial Center that they heard a few people in my community also had family from Lodz, Poland. So I got their contact information and spoke to the 2G (Second Generation family member). He told me his father was from Lodz and some survivors of Lodz put together books and added any photos they had to the book. Well I began a desperate search to find these books. They were not at book stores, at Amazon or anywhere I thought. Next I went to the Library at the Holocaust Memorial Center in West Bloomfield. I asked Feiga if she knew of these books and she was unsure. She searched and brought up hard copies of books on Lodz. I told her they were soft copies and there was a series of them. Well, sure enough she found them.

As I scanned through the book I noticed a genealogist from Lodz was cited in there. He had an email address. I thought perhaps I would reach out to him and see if he could find a little bit more information on my family. I felt confident that I found as much as I could on my mother. I asked if he could find anything else on my mother and asked if he could find anything on my father Bernard Klisman/Benek Klizman from Sosnowiec.

He started whetting my appetite with a few emails on my family. I asked him about the price of his research and he said it depended on how much time he put into it and how much traveling he would have to do. He lived in Piotrkow, Mom's birthplace and did a lot of research in Lodz (which was 15 kilometers away). He threw out a few figures, "Anywhere from $200 USD to $400 USD."

I was skeptical so I told him I would think about it. Well, each day he would send me another email with fascinating information about my family, such as my mother's 2nd grade report card in Piotrkow, a name of her classmates, her families addresses before they moved to Lodz, and more. OK it was hook, line and sinker.

I hired him and each day I received more and more information on my mother's side of the family. I found out not only the names of family members, but their height and weight. I found out how much zlotys they contributed to their Jewish Community. I found out who my grandparents and great grandparents were on both sides of the family. He found out who additional family members were.

He sent me documentation that my father and his two brothers were planning to move to Bolivia. This was an "Emigration Service document" or "Index card." He gave me exact birth dates of family. I was fascinated and intrigued with all this information. It was addicting. I felt like I was on the TV show that traces your family's roots. I felt as if I hit the gold mine again. Unfortunately to get my father's information he would have to take a train, stay in a hotel and then go through the city archives. That may be a future project!

It was as if this was my dissertation. I had acquired a great deal of information. I started sharing this information with my family. I sent an invitation online for them to follow the Ellis/Klisman family tree. Everyone was fascinated because none of us had this family ancestry information.

One day, I called my mother and asked if she would like to go to Poland. Her answer was a firm No. I asked her again but her answer was always "No. Why would I go back there? There were horrible things that happened there. My family died there. There is no one left there from my family."

She always said she had a loving family but unfortunately circumstances were horrific there. I asked her if she would go back if she knew where her mother was buried? She said there were hundreds or thousands that died each day and she did not know what they did with the bodies. I told her that her mother and Moszek were buried in the New Lodz Cemetery. She asked "How could you know that?"

That was when I told her about all the information that is now available online. She said you would have to be 100% accurate that you knew where they were. My sister-in-law Anne and I asked if, even if it was not 100% certain of the exact spot, but if we knew which cemetery they were in, would she go. She said she wasn't sure. Well I told her that there were about 5 different times that I found the exact documentation on various websites that confirmed the spot where her mother and brother were buried. My mother said, "How is that possible?"

After explaining that the Nazis made the Jewish prisoners bury the bodies in the ghetto fields, which was still in the Lodz ghetto, she started thinking this could be a possibility.

Next I contacted the head of the Lodz Cemetery, Agnieska, and asked if anyone there could take a photo of the exact sites for my grandmother and Mom's brother. I checked my email daily for weeks and months and there was no response. One morning, at 6:00 a.m. I was getting ready for work. As always I checked my email. There it was—a vast area of green pasture. It looked bare and unkempt. I realized that was the exact spot that my grandmother was. She was there and no one knew about her or my uncle in over 77 years. No one ever went there to honor her or my uncle's memory. No one knew two beautiful people existed there. There in the ghetto fields there were over 43,000 buried and only approximately 200 graves. At that point I showed the email to my mother and she said she would like to put up a tombstone. She wanted one beautiful tombstone in my grandmother's exact spot to honor the whole Tajch family.

The research began at home on what to put on the tombstone. What would it look like? What could possibly be said on the tombstone to honor such a beautiful family that perished during such horrific times? Agnieska worked with Anne via the email to make sure Liba Rozrawska Tajch, Icek Berek Tajch, Israel Tajch and Moszek Tajch would be remembered forever. A Jewish tombstone was created in Poland. Now it was time to plan our journey to Poland.

IN LOVING MEMORY OF

LIBA
ROZRAZOWSKA
TAJCH
25. 08. 1941

TAJCH FAMILY
ICEK BEREK TAJCH
ISRAEL SRULEK TAJCH
MOSZEK TAJCH

Mom decided to put up one tombstone for the whole family at the site of her mom, Liba. We also put "Loving parents and loving brothers Perished in the Holocaust."

Chapter 14 Our Journey To Poland

    Planning needed to be done. When do we go, who will be our tour guide, who will be our driver, where do I find a tour company, how long do we stay, where in Poland should we go and on and on. The thought of planning such an amazing journey needed a lot of thought. I began by calling tour companies. The majority of them did not return my phone calls. I thought I would go to the Holocaust Memorial Center and interview a staff member there who took this journey with her mother and find out where she went and where she stayed. She gave me names of some hotels she stayed at in various towns. I also joined "Second generation Holocaust Survivors" and other Facebook groups on the Holocaust and asked if anyone went to Poland and if so what hotels they would recommend. I also asked if they knew of any drivers. Well one tour group "Alleyet Tours" called back and was willing to take on this challenge, but then I never heard back from the travel agent. I called again and when she returned the call several days later, she said she had an emergency and thanked me for being so patient. Well patient I was not.

    As a result of not being patient, Anne and I began planning our trip. We decided which cities to go to. I checked with Dr. Weissberg, a man who travels several times a year with tour groups to Poland. He recommended the route we should take after I told him which cities we wanted to see. We decided we would start in Warsaw, the Capital of Poland. From there we would have a driver take us to Lodz. After staying in Lodz a few days we would see Mom's city where she was born, Piotrkow. We would stay in Piotrkow a half day and then travel to my dad's home town of Sosnowiec. After an afternoon in Sosnowiec we would travel in the evening to Krakow. We would stay overnight there and then begin in the morning to see Auschwitz. We would then stay overnight in Krakow and explore the medieval town the next day. The following day we wanted to see the beautiful ski resort in the Tatra Mountains called Zakopane. After exploring Zakopane we would go back to Warsaw.

    Now that the cities were finalized we needed to start calling Expedia and inquire about hotels in several cities in Poland. Many of these hotels in the Jewish quarters were already booked. I wondered who goes to Poland. Why would these hotels be booked? We tried to contact a few online and I called a few directly. Finally Expedia was able to find us a hotel that was on our original list of desired hotels in each city. We booked Hampton Inn by Hilton in Warsaw, the Novotel Hotel in Lodz, the Ester Hotel in Krakow, and back to the Hilton by Hampton Inn by the airport in Warsaw. Thank g-d we had hotels. Now we needed to book our airfare. We got airfare via Air Canada on July 7, 2016 from Metro Detroit, to Toronto and from Toronto to Warsaw. Our return flight was set on July 16, 2016 from Warsaw to Chicago and then Chicago back to Detroit. Finally, with these major events booked, it was time to think about excursions.

What highlights should we see in each town? Thanks to the genealogist we knew we had to see where our parents lived, where Mom was sent to live in the Lodz ghetto, and one of the concentration camps where she and my father were sent. I also wanted to see their school, see where the Jews were deported from (train stations), see some of the highlights of the city, go to synagogues, go to cemeteries, and walk in the footsteps where my family walked. We knew this was going to be a personalized or customized tour that no travel agent could plan. In retrospect, it worked out well that we were planning our journey. I also thought it would be helpful to go to travel advisors and see what the top 10 sites were to see or do in each town. Travel advisors endorsed Viator tours and as a result of that I booked some excursions with this company. They were dependable and exceeded my expectations.

Some of the tours I booked with them were the Jewish Warsaw Tour in Retro cars, the Auschwitz museum, and Zakopane. Some of the tours we booked on our own that were exceptional were Schindler's Factory in Krakow, the Polin Museum in Warsaw, the golf cart tours of the Jewish Quarters, the Schindler's factory and the Old City in Krakow. We also saw the Manufaktura in Lodz and Poznanski's palace in Lodz, and the Survivor's park in Lodz. It was also helpful to have the genealogist Jacek be our tour guide for part of Lodz and Piotrkow.

Some of the best and magical moments were those unplanned and spontaneous such as meeting up with a group of 39 young professionals from J.Roots (in New York) with their Rabbi/Professor in Piotrkow right in front of the synagogue, and what transpired with them in Lodz the next day. Another magical moment was what took place in Lodz Cemetery by our new friends Lila and Jim Tinkoff. Sometimes being in the right place at the right time makes for magic as you will soon find out in the coming chapters and other times being in the wrong place at the wrong time (Jews in Poland) can be an atrocity. One never knows what is in store. I was hoping there would not be any incidents of anti-Semitism on this trip; but never did I imagine some beautiful events would occur spontaneously.

Part V: Genealogy Research & Notes
Chapter 15 Highlights Of Email Correspondences With The Genealogist

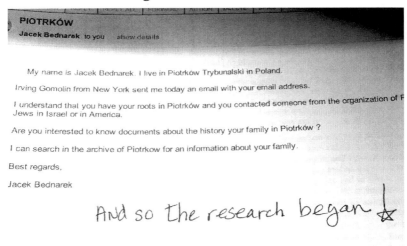

And so the research began ☆

3-10-2016

After reviewing the Hedim/Voice newsletter on Piotrkow, Poland, I was fortunate to come across the name of a genealogist from Piotrkow. When I decided to take a chance on emailing him I did not know how well his English was, if he would be of any help, etc. I told him I was interested in researching my mother who was from his hometown and my father. Before agreeing to work with him, he started corresponding with me on a fairly regular basis in 2016. These were quick responses with enticing information. It became more fascinating with each email. He was confident that he could find more information. So Jacek Bednarek became my connection to all my questions. He had an expertise in research. He was fluent in 6 languages and had traveled to Israel several times. I was quite impressed that although he was not Jewish he spoke Hebrew.

Jacek had excellent skills in acquiring foreign language, doing genealogy research and I picture much more. When my family met with him for brunch I was struck by the fact that he did not drive. He typically rides his bike, but his bike was stolen prior to our meeting. He had to take a bus to come to brunch. He had a desire to go on and on about genealogy, which was wonderful for me. Once he took us to the civil offices for additional documentation on the Tajch family, he became a madman going through the microfiche. I loved watching his intensity and desire to find literature. He found it in record breaking time.

When he joined us in Piotrkow he seemed to just want to show us the old synagogue which is currently the library. He seemed upset when my brother, Mark started talking to another group with a Rabbi. He just wanted to give us the tour and not be bothered with others. Luckily for us, we engaged with the Rabbi and this is where my mother presented her life story to approximately 39 young Jewish professionals from New York (J.Roots).

After that he took us downstairs in the library and showed us the Torah on the wall with bullet holes. He was nothing but wonderful and knowledgeable with my family. Without his guidance, our trip would not have been nearly as informative or personal. He made it feel like he was family when he was in the van with us and told us where to turn to see my mother's family's residence. He was certainly familiar with where we lived from all his research. He impressed me because he did not have documents such as our addresses in front of him, but knew it by memory. I believe he had a photographic memory and we were blessed to have his expertise on this trip.

Some of the highlights that he shared with me were as follows:

- My grandfather Icek Berek Tajch resided at Sierdakza Street, 8. His previous address was Przedborska Street, 8. He knew when the street names changed. He knew his weight was 47 kg., his height was only 152 cm. and the dimension of his chest was 90/82 cm. He was unable to serve in the military because his left leg was 8 cm shorter than his right. What a blessing that he found this information. It makes me feel more connected to my grandfather. Not only do I have a name, but now I can visualize him. I know he resembled his brother Izrael and I have a picture of Izrael. Thanks to Jacek, we drove by this address. There was a large home on that spot. I understand at the time my grandfather lived there, there was a different dwelling there, but how surreal to drive by and walk in that exact spot.

- Jacek also found the registration of the birth of Icek Berek (Beer) Tajch. It was in Russian. His parents were Moszek (29 years old in 1893) and Chana, nee Guderman (25 years old). I was fortunate to work with a man, Sam Shvartzman, at Royal Oak High School. He was born in the Ukraine but fluent in Russian. He was able to transcribe the document.

- Jacek told us that Estera Rajzla Tajch, my mother's older sister who passed away before my mother was born was a twin of Israel. They were born on 15 May, 1917 in Piotrkow. She died in Piotrkow on 20 July, 1926. She was only 9 years old. My mother never knew there were twins in her family.

- There were three Zysla's in my mother's family. My mother, her grandmother, and then her great-great grandmother. Lewek Hajman and Hinda Filipowicz were married. Lewek's parents were Jakub and Zysla.

- Jacek filled in many people in my family tree. He stated my great-grandparents were Moszek Sucher Tajch and Chana Tajch, nee Huberman. Their children were:
  - Blima born on 27 December, 1886 (She was married to a man from the commune of Topolice, about 40 km east of Piotrkow.)
  - Icek Berek born on 14 May, 1889
  - Rajzla born on 18 January, 1891
  - Jenta born on 12 May, 1902 (Spouse was Jakob Wolf Brygier)
  - Chaja Hinda born on 18 November, 1903
  - Gitla born on 12 May, 1905. She died in 1917.

  Information on additional family members is on Ancestry.com

- Kopel Rozrazowski and Estera Rajzla were married. Now I understand why Icek and Liba had a daughter named Estera

Rajzla. Well the older Estera was my great-great grandmother. They had a lot of children! They are all on the family tree.

- Szajndla Rozrazowska (My grandmother's sister) married Zelik Bialowas. Rumor has it they moved to Paris and then got a divorce. They had two girls. Unfortunately, neither Jacek nor I could find any information on Szajndla. Surprisingly when I did a search on Tajch I came across Jewish gen the Holocaust Global Registry that Felicia filled out. She stated that Szajndla immigrated to France in 1923-1926. Her last known address was Paris, France, 129 B.D. Villete Paris X.

Paris 1925 (wikimedia)

Part VI: On Traveling To Poland 2016

Chapter 16 Daily Diary/Blogs

June 2016

Hello everyone.
 I am now getting ready for my adventure to Poland with the family. I am excited to blog all my adventures.

July 5, 2016

This is two days prior to my trip and I am feeling both excitement and trepidation. The tombstone turned out perfectly and I showed it to Mom today. She said it makes her feel good because her family will not be forgotten. I cannot wait to be there and see it in person. The Rabbi will meet us there and say Kaddish and a Hebrew Remembrance prayer. It is also sad that Aunt Felicia passed away right before our trip. She would have loved to have seen photos and hear about our trip.

 I just found out that July 7th through July 9th, President Obama will be in Warsaw for his final summit with NATO leaders. I am anticipating extremely tight security, road closures and some major delays as a result of this.

 As I was packing I found a dime in my suitcase. It was sitting inside of my bag. This was one of many magical moments that was going to happen on this trip. The dime signifies a grandparent is watching over me. Let this emotional and spiritual journey begin. I am ready!

 Also today Mom met with another survivor and dear friend, Leo Beals. He is 94. All the survivors are getting up there in the years. Let's hope they continue to feel good and live a long healthy life!

4,456 Miles

Sophie with Leo Beals

July 7 and 8, 2016

Photo taken by Robert Kiger

Lori and her husband Jeff, my mother, Sophie, my brother Mark and my sister-in-law Anne arrived at Detroit Metro Airport at 3:00 p.m. and found out our 6:20 p.m. flight was delayed three times until 7:45 p.m. We were not sure if we would make our connecting flight from Toronto to Warsaw. We got a wheelchair for Mom and Jeff ran and pushed her while the rest of us ran on the conveyer belts, whenever possible to our gate. We got to the gate during the boarding process. We made it.

We arrived in Warsaw's Chopin Airport at 12:20 p.m. their time. We saw three Air Force one planes labeled "United States of America" at the Chopin Airport so we knew President Barack Obama had arrived. We also knew his secret service men and their vehicles had arrived as well.

Much to my surprise, President Obama was staying across the street from our hotel at the Marriott. Jeff, Mark and Anne stopped in and spoke to secret service. They asked where the President was. After the secret service inquired who they were and why they were there, he then informed him the President would be back in one half hour to three hours. He stated "You are welcome to wait." Jeff asked if he could be photographed with the President and he responded "The President has been taking pictures with people." Since we had a full agenda planned that day, Jeff, Mark and Anne decided to leave the Marriott.

Since Obama and many other top officials were in Poland for the NATO meeting the roads were filled with "Policiza" on every corner on many streets. We knew the motorcades would be passing through shortly due to the road closures and high security. Sure enough we heard the sirens blaring and several cars whizzing by.

WARSAW, Poland (July 8, 2016) Secretary of Defense Ash Carter poses for a photo with NATO ministers of defense at the 2016 NATO summit in Warsaw, Poland July 8, 2016. **(DoD photo by Navy Petty Officer 1st Class Tim D. Godbee)(Released) (wikimedia)**

There were 28 heads of state and heads of government from different countries invited to participate in the NATO (North Atlantic Treaty Organization) Warsaw Summit Meeting on July 8–9, 2016. This was the 27th meeting. It took place at the National Stadium in Warsaw. Countries included Albania, Belgium, Bulgaria, Canada, Croatia, Czech Rep, Denmark, Estonia Greece, France, Germany, Iceland, Latvia, Lithuania, Luxembourg, Italy, Hungary,

Netherlands, Portugal, Slovakia, Slovenia, Spain, Norway, Romania, Poland, USA, Turkey, and the United Kingdom.
According to the USNEWS.com they met to discuss 10 goals:
- Send four battalions to Poland and the Baltics.
- Expand activities in migrant crisis,
- Keep an open door.
- Reaffirm commitment to Afghanistan
- Augment role in Islamic State group fight
- Contribute to stability of Libya
- Emphasize cyber threats
- Deepen ties with Finland and Sweden
- Enhance capacity-building in Ukraine
- Create allied Black Sea fleet

    We checked in to the beautiful Hilton Hampton by Warsaw Inn. It had all the modern conveniences of any hotel in the USA. Free WIFI, computers in the lobby, a restaurant and more. This is where we met Lilia and Jim in the elevator. Jeff mentioned we should explore the synagogue and they mentioned they would be going to services there in the evening. We asked where they were from and why they were in Poland. Lilia stated she was born in Lodz after the war and her uncle was a survivor as well as another family member. She wanted to see Poland, then go to Prague and end up in Israel. She told us she was a Hebrew School teacher in Florida. She mentioned she was going to go to Lodz on a tour on Monday.

    My mother explained we were going to go to Lodz on Sunday at 11:00 a.m. to meet a Rabbi there and have a service for her family that perished in the ghetto and camps. She was welcome to join us. Soon we felt bonded to people who were once strangers. It was hard to believe within a few minutes there was a connection there. She knew one of my mother's friends who lived in Florida. They belong to the same congregation there. Little did we know that Lila and Jim would do something so moving for us on Sunday, July 9th, 2016 that will never be forgotten?

    We decided to explore Warsaw. It was a very cosmopolitan looking city. There were beautiful high rise buildings and it was a bustling city. I saw McDonald's, H & M clothing store, a Deloitte CPA firm, beautiful malls and more. We saw many young people on the streets walking and eating outdoors. My mother said "It is hard to believe that I am in Poland now. Pinch me"

    I was wondering if there were going to be any signs that there was a war in Warsaw. Is the city camouflaged from the past? Much of Warsaw was rebuilt after the war.

Exterior and interior of the synagogue in the city center of Warsaw.

We went to the City Center and that is where we saw a beautiful synagogue still in existence there. It was hard to believe this was not destroyed by the war, while most of the city was in rubbles. Mark, Anne and Jeff walked in to the synagogue and my mother was tired, so we went back to the hotel to rest. It was not easy

Chopin Museum (wikimedia)

4,456 Miles

getting back since several of the streets were shut down to the police barricading the roads. Jeff purchased a beautiful wooden rabbi statue for me. They headed back to the hotel and the group was going to go to service in the evening at the same Synagogue.

We decided we would like to check out Chopin's museum. We hopped in a Mercedes Benz vehicle and much to our surprise the driver took us to Fryderyk Chopin's home, his university and then to the museum. It was so exciting to see where he grew up and learn about his life.

That evening the whole group went for service at the Synagogue. It was a very moving Orthodox service. Because it was Orthodox, the men were sitting downstairs while the women were sitting upstairs. It was almost surreal that we were participating in services in Poland just like my grandparents used to do with my parents. Many of the members were Jewish foreigners sightseeing or doing what we were doing, visiting their roots. I was told there were 647 members.

This is where we reconnected with Jim and Lila, whom we met earlier in the elevator of our hotel. Lilia sat with us. My mother also met another women whose mother was from her home town, Lodz. This woman lives in France. She stated there is anti-Semitism in France now but she lives with the Aristocrats so it does not affect her. The service was beautiful and I am so glad my mother and the rest of the family could see that there still is a hint of Judaism in Warsaw.

Here we are in the city center of Warsaw in July 2016

We ate at a lovely outdoor restaurant in Warsaw that served authentic food. I ordered pierogies and they were delicious. They have many different styles of pierogies such as meat, potatoes and more. It was so reasonable too! Too bad these weren't the living conditions for my parents, grandparents and great-grandparents years ago. It still is so hard to fathom how horrible living was back in Poland in the time my family lived there. We headed back to the hotel and I was anxious to write in my blog of Poland so I could share my daily experiences with my children, niece and nephew, and cousins. I wanted them to be able to live vicariously through my experiences even if they were not with me on this crazy journey.

July 9, 2016

Today we went on the Jewish Heritage tour of the Warsaw ghetto. We rode in our retro taxis. No seat belts, but I guess that was not law back then. Marcin, our driver, was great. I love the name because it reminded me of one of my students that I saw at school, who happened to be from my dad's home town of Sosnowiec.

Here we are in our retro taxi!

The Warsaw ghetto placed the Jewish population (approximately 400,000 Jews) within the closed walls and then added an additional 100,000 Jews who were from outside of Warsaw. Brick walls with barbed wire prevented the Jews from leaving the ghetto. There were bullet holes in the wall from the Jewish Uprising in April 1943 and the Partisans Uprising in April 1944.

4,456 Miles

There were no Gypsies or Poles there, only Jews. Many were murdered there. Almost all of the remaining inhabitants were sent to the death camp of Treblinka. It took 52 days to transport thousands of Jews to the death camps.

Look at the bullet holes in the wall behind us. The only building to survive in the rubble was the Catholic Church because this was where the Nazis stored the Jewish possessions. In this photo are Anne and Mark Klisman, Sophie Tajch Klisman, and Lori and Jeff Ellis

We walked the path to the UmSchlagplatz, where the people were crowded into cattle cars to their death. We saw names of those who have perished on the walls of this monument. The walls were shaped in the form of a Jewish tombstone with pictures of trees on the top. There were yahrzeit candles lit as we went to this area. The pain and suffering can still be felt as I walked in the exact pathway as others took seventy plus years ago.

Facts about Warsaw: 100,000 Jews perished of starvation and disease. Almost all others were transported to the death camp Treblinka. We walked the path to the UmSchlagplatz, where the people were crowded into cattle cars to their death.

Next Marcin took us to the famous Mila 18 site which was the headquarters of the Jewish Underground and the bunker where the Jews fought the Nazis. They killed approximately 300 Nazis. The ruins of the bunker at Mila 18 Street was the final resting place of the commanders and fighters of the Jewish Combat organization. On May 8, 1943 surrounded by Nazis after 3 weeks of struggle, many

Lori Klisman Ellis

Above: Mila 18, the headquarters of the Jewish Underground and the bunker where the Jews who survived the Uprising chose to end their own lives instead of having the Nazis do it. "Life without freedom was nothing"

were weak and suffering from starvation. The Nazis came back with more soldiers and ammunition to fight. With no equal fight possible, many of the resistance fighters took their own lives. "Life without Freedom was nothing."

Next we went to visit apartment or building 28 in Warsaw. Emanuel Ringelblum was a historian and hid chronicles of life in the ghetto in three places. This spot, apartment 28, marks the exact place where one set of archives was found underground. There is another set believed to be under what is now the Chinese Embassy but China will not give permission to search for it.

Historian Emanuel Ringelblum hid chronicles of life in the ghetto in three places. Apartment 28 (photo left) marks the spot where one of these sets of papers were found underground. (Photo right is from Wikimedia—public domain.)

4,456 Miles

We also saw a monument of a sewer. This is where the brave Jews climbed in to procure weapons, food and supplies. Jews who aided in the 1943 uprising escaped through the sewer as well and many of them went on to fight in the 1944 uprising. Eventually the Nazis' realized that some of the Jews were escaping through the sewers and so they poisoned the water to kill them.

Photo of the monument to the brave Jews who used the sewers to procure weapons, food and supplies.

We went to the Polin Museum to experience the 1,000 year history of the Polish Jews. This building was established in 2005 and did not open until April 2013. They have close to a half of a million visitors each year. This museum was created on the exact site of the former Jewish ghetto in Warsaw. The outside of the building was created on a slant to represent the parting of the red sea. This museum has won awards for its outstanding contribution. We had a spectacular docent who was so well informed about every part of this museum. There were so many intriguing parts to this museum. We saw the Forest, the Middle-Ages, the Jewish life in the 15th and 16th centuries, the Jewish town in the 17th and 18th centuries, the modern life of the Jews in the 19th century, the Jewish Street, the Holocaust and the Post War. There was a gorgeous replica of a bema from the Gwozdziec Synagogue and the celestial canopy. It was breathtaking. I felt as if I was in a synagogue during that era. This museum is a must to see for every Jew around the world!

Entrance to the Polin Jewish Museum

Here is a monument of the ghetto heroes. The original monument is in Yad Vashem and this is a replica of it. Left to right: Jeff and Lori Ellis, Sophie Tajch Klisman, Mark and Anne Klisman.

On the outside of this museum there is a monument to the ghetto heroes. The original monument is in Yad Vashem, Israel, and this is a replica. The stone was purchased by Hitler to represent his expected victory, but in the end it was used to mark the victory of the Jews! On the back of the monument there is a carving of a burning ghetto. There is a mother with a child on it. Every year there is a big march which the president of Poland attends. The symbol on the back represents people walking slowly on the road to their death. Our tour guide shared "To save one Jew from the ghetto it took 15–20 people to make this happen." This monument represents the fight for freedom and dignity in Poland as well as in other countries around the world.

We also saw the statue of Karski (Jan Romuald Kozielewski) sitting on the bench at the Polin Museum. He was a courier for the Polish Underground. One of his missions was to get evidence of Nazi atrocities. He was one of the men who went down the sewer into the ghetto to record what he saw. Afterwards he met with Franklin D. Roosevelt (the President at that time) and others to try to persuade them to stop the atrocities. The President did not intervene and Karski's message was not believed and ignored. Karski wrote a book documenting his experiences called *Courier from Poland: The Story of a Secret State* to inform everyone on what was transpiring to try to sway public opinion.

After the war, he became a Professor of Georgetown University. Karski was nominated twice for the Noble Prize but never received it. He felt like a failure his whole life since he could not convince Western powers to rescue Jews from mass murder by the Nazis.

Also, near this bench was an oval shape monument on the ground which represents an entrance to the sewers. It had an olive on it to represent peace. There were some other symbols as well.

Warsaw was brought down to rubbles during WW2. What remained was one beautiful church, which the SS purposefully preserved in order to secure Jewish possessions there. In 2004 Warsaw joined the Eastern Union and at that time Warsaw began to build new and beautiful buildings.

We did observe some anti-government protests going on the day we visited Warsaw. People were protesting the government's attempts to control the judicial branch. Although peaceful, it was still quite a large gathering.

July 10, 2016

Today was the most anticipated day of our journey. Today we met with Kasha, our young Polish driver who would be doing this type of work for the very first time. We got her name from a colleague from Uncle Rick. His colleague was born in Poland and had some connections. We took a chance with her and hoped she would be dependable. There was a lot of correspondence in advance about where she would be driving us and making sure she rented the van in her name. Well luckily she came on time, or actually early. She met us at our hotel as planned. Kasha frightened me initially by stating the van she requested was gone so she would have to learn how to drive an automatic. She has always driven a tiny car with a stick shift so this was going to be a challenge. Her dad begged her not to drive and worried about her driving if there was a storm in our upcoming route. Thank goodness she took this challenge and was a safe and dependable driver. She soon learned driving an automatic was much easier than driving a stick shift.

Our plan at this point was to be at the Lodz Cemetery at 11:00 a.m. promptly to meet Agnieska and the Rabbi. Many emails and phone calls occurred before this point so I was confident all would go smoothly. Also I heard the car ride was estimated to be an hour and a half, but we allowed two hours and forty-five minutes in case there would be traffic or trouble finding the entrance to the cemetery. The journey went smoothly but it was a bit challenging finding the entrance to the cemetery which is 96 acres in size.

Agnieska said she would show up on her day off on Sunday, so she could get paid of course, to guide us to the new Tajch tombstone. She was there waiting for us. She was a very warm and helpful women. Her husband took care of the grounds so that the tombstone would look beautiful in that spot: U=VI Row 5: Grave 480 Left side.

Lori Klisman Ellis

Today we arrived at the Lodz Jewish cemetery. Seeing the tombstone in the exact spot where Liba (my grandmother) was buried was extremely emotional!! Mom finally got a chance to thank her for her life and being a wonderful mother. She introduced Mark, Anne, Lori and Jeff to her. She spoke about her grandchildren! There was not a dry eye there.

While we waited for the Rabbi by the red building I saw a beautiful butterfly circling over our head. I immediately felt comforted and thought our grandparents were looking over us.

Well 11:00 turned to 11:10 then 11:20 and still no Rabbi. But to our surprise our friend Lila and Jim Tinkoff and their tour guide appeared. Lila comforted us by letting us know she was a Hebrew School teacher and knew the blessings. Luckily, as a back-up, I brought a copy of the remembrance prayer and the Kaddish prayer. After emailing the Rabbi, his wife wrote back that there were some circumstances and that if we still needed him he would attend in 45 minutes or in the afternoon. So with much frustration and disappointment we made a decision to proceed without him.

To our surprise Lila was fabulous. She sang the prayers and we joined in on Kaddish. Jeff and Mark read the English version of the prayers as well.

Lilia and Jim Tinkoff with Sophie in 2016

4,456 Miles

My mother spoke to her mother in Polish and understandably became extremely emotional. Can you imagine speaking to the soul of your mother whom you have not spoken to in 77 years? This was beyond painful yet beautiful. She finally got a chance to thank her for her life and for being a wonderful mother. We all spoke to her. I thanked her for giving me the most kind and loving mother ever. I told her I wished I could have met her and I know I would have loved her. I wish I could have met the whole family. Mark and Anne spoke to her as well. Anne thanked her for sacrificing her bread to give to my mother who was starving. She was a selfless and loving human. The thought of losing her life at the age of 51 is absurd.

After a few hours we meandered to Mom's brother's exact burial spot. Moszek was merely 17 years old when he died. I took out the photo that I had of him on my phone and we all cried. It was a painful day.

I still question how could there be a G-d if something so devastating like this happened. With all the pain and suffering, I was hoping this was a little closure for my mother.—finally coming to the realization that her family will have a beautiful and proper service—they will never be forgotten. The video and pictures we took that day will be treasured for a lifetime and passed down from one generation to the next. We love you Tajch family. You are in our thoughts and heart forever.

When asked if Mom was ready to leave she said she never wanted to leave and that she could stay there forever. How heart wrenching!!

Prior to going to the Tajch tombstone, we walked into the funeral home (Beit Tahara) at the Lodz Cemetery briefly. This was founded in 1896. This is located at ul. Bracka and Zmienna. To the right of it was a monument to the victims of the Holocaust. Unfortunately we were so anxious to get to the Tajch tombstone that we did not see the Holocaust monument in the Lodz Cemetery. After searching for a photo of this I came across a message that was written on this monument. It stated:

> "To the Jews of Lodz
> Who were murdered by
> the barbarian German Nazis
> In the years 1939-1945
> In ghettos and camps
> In eternal memory!"
> The Jews of the City of Lodz
> VIII 1947

There was also another memorial plaque that read
**"For world remembrance
Of innocent Jewish victims of Lodz
And surrounding areas
Murdered by the Nazis
In ghettos and camps
During the years 1939-1945
May they be forever remembered in our hearts."**

As we walked one could not help but notice the ginormous monument of the Poznanski's family. It was larger than life. It matched the magnitude of his palace. It was definitely something to see. Along the path to get to the Tajch tombstone we saw many old and unkempt areas. The tombstones looked eerie. The initial part of our walk to our family's tombstone looked like a scene from a horror show or spooky Halloween scene.

We were also in the ghetto field in the Lodz cemetery. This is where the deaths occurred between the years of 1940–1944. They estimated there to be 43,000 burials. The Germans did not allow stone grave markers and so metallic plates or metal bed frames were put up. More recently a project was done by Israelis to put low concrete marker on the grave sites in the ghetto field. Today (July 10th, 2016), there are approximately 200 tombstones within the 43,000 graves in the ghetto field.

When we were getting ready to leave the Lodz cemetery, Lila, Jim and their tour guide told us they did not have a ride. When Lila hired the tour guide she did not know that in Europe you need to hire a separate driver. Lucky for us, we had a driver but no tour guide. We also had a van for 7 with only 6 of us. We actually squeezed in 3 more and prayed that we would not get pulled over and ticketed. So now we had a tour guide and they wanted to go to Radegast Railway Station to see where the Jews were forced into the trains heading towards the death camps and concentration camps. I thought it would be too much for my mother, so I kept offering to drop Mom and I off at the hotel to rest and let the rest of them see this museum. Mom was determined to keep up with what the group wanted so sure enough she put on her tough appearance and off we went to Radegast.

In January, 1942 through August, 1944 the Germans deported Jews and others from the Lodz ghetto to various concentration camps via the Radegast Railway Station. All that was left from my family to transport were Mom, her sister Aunt Felicia and one brother Israel. They were transported to Auschwitz. Mom

4,456 Miles

Next we went to Radegast Railway Station where my mother, Aunt Felicia and their brother Srulek Israel were forced into cattle cars headed to Auschwitz. My mother showed such strength here!

learned that at the Radegast Railway Station they measured people there and that helped to determine where they would be sent. There were close to 200,000 Jews from Lodz left from the ghetto. There are large signs designed in the shape of a Jewish Headstone conveying various destinations such as Auschwitz, Chelmon, Ravenbruck and more.

There are exhibitions in this museum one being Mom's Lodz ghetto exhibition from 1940–1944. There were books at the table documenting the exact date, time and passenger and where they sent them. Each day states names in alphabetical order. There were no books from Lodz dating back to 1944. The docent said by that time they had so many passengers going through and they could not keep up anymore with the documentation. What an eerie feeling that would have been to see the family's names in these books. For some visitors it would be so helpful to know where their loved one was heading.

Another exhibition there was the "Kufer Rodziny Schwarz" exhibit. There is a suitcase which was in the attic of a building on Organizacji Win Street. The suitcase belonged to the Schwarz family which may have perished in the camps.

My mother was amazingly strong as she walked through this exhibition. She asked the docent questions. She chose not to enter the cattle cars which was understandable. She did read out loud that the sign said no more than 20 passengers and stated there were 100 to 200 people crammed into these box cars without windows, with no food, drinks, seats or bathroom facilities. She said they were treated worse than animals. She also chose not to enter the train station which displayed a wall full of photographs. It is hard to believe we walked in the spot where her family walked. It is still surreal that being the youngest sibling in her family that she along with her sister survived. Were they the strongest, smartest, luckiest? What allowed them to survive and have the will to live? Was it having each other? Was it fate? We will never know these answers but I am so blessed that she survived! If the whole family perished who would honor their memory?

Later on, we checked into Novotel Hotel in Lodz and ate at the mall. In the evening we located the area where Mom lived. It was painful to see the run down area and decrepit conditions. One residence was Reiter Strauss 13 flat 1. Building 13 was missing but we saw building 11 and 15. We met a young couple with a baby entering their apartment in building 11. Mom asked if they were aware that this used to be a ghetto and they said yes. I wanted to see their place but we never asked to go up!

4,456 Miles

Beautiful ornate churches and buildings in Lodz.

Our driver Kasha and Anne Klisman posing at the Anatewka restaurant. The restaurant specializes in Jewish cuisine and is filled with memorabilia.

July 11, 2016

Today we had the day to explore Lodz. I asked to meet with Jacek, our genealogist. He joined us for breakfast at the Novotel Hotel. I soon realized he would be a gift to me and my family. He had high intellectual cognitive skills and recalled a great deal of information on my family. He was a bit difficult to understand when he spoke in English, perhaps due to his foreign dialect, and not a lot of inflection and loudness to his voice.

Jacek needed to go to the synagogue to get some documents signed for some clients so I offered him a ride in our van. He directed Kasha to the Reicher Synagogue. It was a former Jewish Community Center and now approximately only 20 people attend services there.

Today we met with Jacek, the genealogist during breakfast. He came with us to a synagogue in Lodz. The Rabbis have been using it as a synagogue for the last 20 years. Prior to that it was used as a Jewish Community Center.

The synagogue was built in 1895–1900 to serve the Reicher family. The owner of the synagogue was forced to go to the Lodz ghetto and soon the synagogue was taken over by a German who happened to be a school friend of Reicher's son. As a result of this, the synagogue was not destroyed by the Nazis. Upon entering the synagogue I tried to envision my grandparents and aunts and uncles entering it on Shabbat and praying there. It had great beauty. It is another sign of victory to know, however few Jews there are, there is still a synagogue standing.

From there we walked to a court house to do a quick search on the Tajch family. Jacek asked for the address of my mother's residence in Lodz and got Microfiche. He was rapidly turning the wheels on the machine until he reached her address. This is where he found the Tajch family registered at Reiter 13 Flat 1, Lodz Poland. Here we found out my Aunt Felicia's birth date was surprisingly different than what my mother thought. Felicia was born in 1919. Knowing that she was three years older made me feel happy to know her longevity. However, there was a feeling of sadness knowing that Aunt Felicia passed away just before our trip and would never be able to hear about our adventure. We found out my Uncle Israel was actually born the same year as my Aunt Estera. They were twins! We found that out from Jacek before the trip. My mother never knew that. My father also had twins on his side of the family. At this point we departed from Jacek and said we would be in Piotrkow tomorrow morning and perhaps we could meet up.

Survivor Park/Marek Eldelman Dialogue Center

We continued on with our journey to see the Survivor's Park, The Marek Eldelman Dialogue Center in Lodz. There was a beautiful monument there shaped in the Star of David. It was created by Czeslaw Bielecki. The walls of this monument had the names of the righteous. It was very moving to see that there were many good Poles who tried to help and save the lives of Jews, even though the Nazis threatened them with death to them and their family. There are many gorgeous trees symbolizing each survivor of Lodz.

We went to the Survivors Park where survivors of Lodz will have a tree planted in honor of them (my mom and aunt). Also a brick with their name will be placed on the ground of the park. Each season we will get a photo of what the tree will looks like.

Granite pavers with names of survivors. We were thrilled to received notice that Sophie and Felicia share a beautiful granite paver!

I had written up a biography on my mom and aunt for this park. Staff will plant one tree for my mother and aunt. Every season we will be emailed a photo of the tree. What a beautiful thing to do, to honor the survivors. I look forward to seeing how beautiful the tree becomes with each passing season; the changing of the colors of the leaves and new buds forming. The new buds may be symbolic of new birth, such as children, grandchildren and hopefully great grandchildren.

Also, a brick with their name will be placed on the ground of the park. I am hopeful that future generations will go and see our family's name and be proud of how they were survivors!

Survivor Park Biographies

This is also called the Mark Edelman Dialogue Center in Lodz. The exact number of survivors of the Lodz ghetto is not known. It is estimated to be between 7 and 12 thousand people. The Survivor's Park is dedicated to those survivors and their memories. A tree was planted for Sophie Tajch Klisman and Felicia Tajch Shloss in 2016. In 2016 we were told that 545 trees were planted and the first one was planted in 2004. What an honor to have a tree planted for the two of them. In addition, there are granite pavers engraved with the name of survivors of Lodz. Now everyone will be able to see their pavers as well. The staff was a pleasure to work with. We were moved by such a beautiful park in memory of all our loved ones that went through such a horrific time in their life.

History of Survivor Park

Survivor Park in Lodz, Poland was initially going to have several trees symbolizing people being led into annihilation. Near the trees was going to be an empty field. The vision was changed by a man named Czeslaw Bielecki. He created a Jewish Star of David and a Polish symbol (a hovering eagle). The Star of David has a horn beam hedge around it. Names of the Polish Righteous are inscribed in the walls of the monument. One can see the monument as it is reflected in the nearby pond. It is a beautiful sight. It is an unbelievable feeling that my mother and aunt will forever be inscribed in the granite pavers and have a tree symbolizing the blooming of their lives.

There is a second stage of the park. It is called the Centre of Dialogue. It is an educational and exposition center. They hold conferences, seminars, workshops and celebrations. If you travel to Poland this is a worthwhile site to see.

Granite Plaque # 608

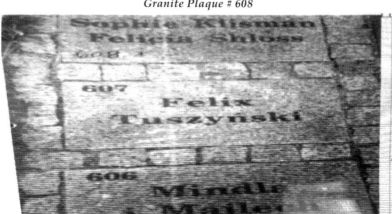

CERTIFICATE

This is to certify that

Sophie Klisman

and

Felicia Shloss

has been assigned
a memorial tree number

608

in **the Survivors' Park**,
which symbolises the saved lives
of those who survived
the Litzmannstadt Getto.

Hanna ZDANOWSKA

Mayor of the City of Lodz

Stories Submitted to Survival Park:
Additional information on Zysla Tajch/Sophie Klisman

STORY OF ZYSLA TAJCH

Zysla Tajch, was one of 5 children from Liba Rozrazowska and Icek Berek Tajch. She was born on July 6, 1929 in Lodz Poland. When she was approximately 10 years old when the war broke out and she along with her family were forced to move to the Litzmannstadt ghetto. This is where she lost her mother Liba, her father Icek Berek and one brother Moszek Tajch due to starvation and other horrific reasons. Later Fajga, her sister Zysla and brother, Izrael Sruelik were transported to Auswitz, where the sisters never saw Izrael Srulek again. The sisters were transported to other horrific concentration camps. Miraculously they were liberated after approximately 5 years. The two sisters survived: Fajga Tajch (Felicia Shloss) and Zysla Tajch (Sophie Klisman).

After the war both went to a Displaced Persons camp in Germany. This is where she had the desire to go back to school and continue her education. Shortly after, she got the news that she along with her sister and her sister's family were allowed to come to America. They went by boat to New York and eventually made their way to Detroit, Michigan. Zysla, also known as Sophie went to night school to pursue her education and then met Bernard Klisman, also a survivor of the Holocaust and they got married.

Sophie worked as a Sales Representative for women's clothing and a fashion consultant. She had two children, Mark and Lori. Mark became a Medical Pathologist and currently recruits Doctors to do their lab work at a hospital he works for. He got married and has two children. Lori is a Speech and Language Pathologist, got married and has two children.

Sophie was a loving wife to her Bernard. He unfortunately suffered from Alzheimer's and passed away two years ago. She is a loving mother and grandmother!

Sophie also spoke often about the atrocities of the Holocaust at the Holocaust Memorial Center in West Bloomfield, MI. in hopes of educating the youth of America! She is a true survivor! My hope is a tree will be planted to honor her as a survivor of the Holocaust.

Submitted by her niece Lori Klisman Ellis

4,456 Miles

STORY OF FIEGA TAJCH

Feiga Tajch, was one of 5 children from Liba Rozrazowska and Icek Berek Tajch. She was born on November 5, 1922 in Lodz Poland. When she was approximately 17 years old when the war broke out and she along with her family were forced to move to the Litzmannstadt ghetto. This is where she lost her mother Liba, her father Icek Berek and one brother Moszek Tajch due to starvation and other horrific reasons. Later Faiga, her sister Zysla and brother Izrael Sruelik were transported to Aushwitz, where the sisters never saw Izrael Sruelek again. The sisters were transported to other horrific concentration camps. Miraculously they were liberated after approximately 5 years. The two sisters survived: Feiga Tajch (Felicia Shloss) and Zysla Tajch (Sophie Klisman).

After the war both went to a Displaced Persons camp in Germany. Felicia got married to another Holocaust survivor Roman Shloss and had a daughter, Loretta in Germany. Eventually they were allowed to come to the United States and went to New York and then made their way to Detroit, Michigan. Felicia and Roman had another daughter, Marla in Detroit. Both daughters were educated and married. Loretta was a Biology teacher, and then an attorney. She got married and had two boys. The boys got married and had two children each. Felicia is a great grand- mother. Marla became a social worker, got married and had one daughter. Her daughter is in college hoping to be a vet. Felicia's husband passed away at approximately 86 years old. Felicia is now living close to her daughter, Loretta in Fort Worth, Texas. She is 93 years old. In her past, Felicia spoke often about the atrocities of the Holocaust in hopes of educating the youth of America! She is a true survivor! My hope is a tree will be planted to honor her as a survivor of the Holocaust.

Submitted by her niece Lori Klisman Ellis

Zysla Tajch, was one of 5 children from Liba Rozrazowska Tajch and Icek Berek Tajch. She was born in July 6, 1929 in Piotrkow, Poland. The family moved to Lodz, Poland. When she was approximately 10 years old the war broke out and she along with her family were forced to move to the Lodz ghetto. This is where she lost her mother Liba, her father, Icek Berek and one brother Moszek due to starvation and other horrific conditions. Later her sister Fajga (Felicia Shloss), Zysla and her brother Izrael were transported by train to Auschwitz. That was the last time they saw their brother. The sisters were then transported to two other concentration camps. Miraculously Sophie and Felicia were liberated after approximately 5 years in the ghetto and camps.

After the war they searched for family, but no one could be found. They both went to a displaced persons camp in Germany. After 5 years they received notification that they could come to America. This is where Zysla/Sophie went to night school to pursue her education. She met another survivor Bernard Klisman and they got married.

Sophie and Bernard worked and raised two children, Mark Klisman and Lori Klisman. Her children got married and shortly after they became a Bubbie and Zayde. Sophie was a loving wife, mother and grandmother. Unfortunately two years ago her husband passed away from Alzheimer's and her sister, Felicia just recently passed away as well. Last year, Sophie became a speaker at the Holocaust Memorial Center to educate the youth about the atrocities of the war. Her daughter-in-law Anne became a docent.

Recently her daughter, Lori began researching her ancestry and came across valuable genealogical information such as the location of Zysla's mother's and brother's exact burial spot. On July 7, 2016 Sophie and her two children and their spouses made the journey back to Poland to retrace her roots. At that time a beautiful tombstone was put up at the Lodz cemetery to honor the memory of the Tajch family. The family visited the location of her homes and concentration camp as well.

For more information on her journey, it can be viewed on their blog **https://ellispoland2016.blogspot.com**

July 11, 2016—in the evening

In the evening we went to visit Charlie Silow's friend, Mirka Gluck at Manufaktura. It is a huge mall now but it used to be a textile manufacturing plant. We admired the grounds. There was a T K Max (Not TJ Max but an identical store). We walked near the volleyball court and pool. We went into the mall briefly and finally we met Mirka at Anatewka restaurant. It was the same restaurant we ate at the other night but at a different location. She was a warm and lovely woman.

Mirka invited us back to her home to meet her husband and three sons. It was fascinating to see how she lives in Lodz. Her home was probably considered spacious for the typical home in Poland. She along with her husband were both highly educated. She was a CPA and her husband was an architect. She provided private tutoring for her boys and gave them the luxury of traveling

We met Charles Silow's good friend Mirka and her family at Manufaktura. It is a huge mall now, but it used to be a textile manufacturing plant. We ate dinner at Anatewka.

4,456 Miles

After that we went to Karol Posnanski's Palace. He was the largest textile manufacturer in all of Poland. We toured his mansion. It is now a museum with artifacts from well-known famous residents of Lodz.

to many different countries. They were all involved in after school events like dance class and sports. She was extremely hospitable and offered delicious desserts and home-made wine to us. This was definitely a highlight of our trip to meet her and her family and to hear the stories she shared.

Mirka invited us over to see her lovely home in Lodz and meet her family.

Both she and her husband thought they were Catholic and many years later found out they were both Jewish. Mirka and her sister were reading a book one day and looking at a picture of a women with thick, black curly hair. Mirka's older sister said that her mom looked like the girl in the book. The girl in the book was Jewish. Her sister asked her mom if she was sure she was not Jewish, not even 50% Jewish. The mom sat the girls down and said that she never wanted to tell them this and said she was 100% Jewish.

The mother was actually raised by a gentile woman because Mirka's grandparents were taken away and murdered in the war.

Kasha, the driver is on the far left. Jeff and Lori Ellis, Sophie Tajch Klisman. Mark Klisman is standing. Anne Klisman and our new friend from Poland, Mirka.

4,456 Miles

Mirka's husband found out years later his grandfather was a popular author of books. His father used a fictitious name, Stanislaw Byrinski, to protect him since he was Jewish. The name Stanislaw Byrinski happened to be the same name as my father's caregiver. It is strange to see how life is interwoven. Is this a coincidence or was this whole trip spiritual?

After that we headed back to the Novotel Hotel in Lodz and I began thinking about tomorrow's journey to my mother's and father's birthplaces.

July 12, 2016

Prior to heading out to Mom's birth place, Piotrkow we made an initial stop at the Andel's by Vienna House Lodz which was originally another textile factory. The motif was very modern and surprisingly the designers kept the original architecture of the factory. There were the original ceilings and more. On the outside of the hotel was a large sculpture of a man in black.

Piotrkow here we come. It was approximately 16 miles away. Jacek gave Kasha his business card with the expectation we would contact him early in the morning. I asked the family if they wanted him to join us. We were limited on time and we knew he liked to get into the history of the town and thus we decided we would manage on our own, without his narration of the town. Well after driving and driving and searching for Mom's home I decided he may be helpful. Now it was 11:00 a.m. and when Kasha contacted him, he was already on the street corner (possibly for two hours) waiting for us. He said he knew we were coming early in the morning and why didn't we call sooner. Anyway, we immediately saw him on the corner and he hopped in. This was the best thing that happened because I asked him to help us find Mom's home.

Today we went to Piotrkow, the city where my mother was born! Jacek the genealogist showed us the spot where my mother lived with her family—it was the brown building, lower level.

He said turn right here, make a left and sure enough he found her address although it did not look familiar to Mom, and it may have been a different building. Her address was Slowaki 7 which is now Kaliska 7. Jacek stated "Your mom was a baby and her dad and the family lived here. Now I know why I couldn't find her home. I was looking for the old street name which had since been changed to Kaliska

4,456 Miles

7. It was a brown building on the lower level. On the top it was a yellowish color. Possibly this was her dwelling. Perhaps it was the original but maybe the color changed. Unfortunately there was no one to validate that this was the original dwelling.

It was hard to believe that this was the exact location where my mother lived with her family. It was hard to believe that we walked in the same places where she and her family lived.

Next we walked into the "Great Synagogue" where her family used to go to pray. Prior to entering something magical happened! We met a group of college students from New York with their Rabbi/professor. They were part of the J.Roots Journey. When Rabbi Schmuel found out Mom was a survivor he asked her to speak to his group. She shared her life story and touched everyone's lives at that moment! She along with the other survivors defeated Hitler! It was an empowering moment to witness by everyone.

We met a group of young adults from New York, who were part of J. Roots, and their Rabbi. When the Rabbi found out Mom was a survivor he asked her to speak to his group. She shared her life story and touched everyone's lives

at that moment. She along with the other survivors defeated Hitler!

Many students were crying and several were videotaping her. She got a standing ovation. They insisted on a photo of the whole group with our family. The students had on their agenda that they would be going to Lodz Cemetery tomorrow to see the graves there. The Rabbi stated now they will visit Liba Tajch and her family. I asked if they could take a photo at that spot. Much to our surprise not only did they take the photo, but the Rabbi also chanted Hebrew prayers there. I do believe her soul rose. The Tajch tombstone was so popular there that weekend! As part of the Jewish tradition, the students and Rabbi put rocks on top of the tombstone to pay their respect and let everyone know they visited. We will cherish the memory and the video.

We walked into the synagogue where her family used to go to pray. Note the bullet holes in the Torah. The Ukrainians shot the remaining Jews from Piotrkow.

Afterward Jacek took us around the synagogue, which is now a library. On the lower level, hidden all the way in the back was a huge and beautiful canvas painting of the Torah. To our surprise it was riddled with bullets, but still hung up. How amazing that it is still on the wall, but unfortunately hidden to most who enter the library.

Jacek shared some interesting information about Piotrkow with us. He stated it was the first ghetto in Poland. The synagogue was 200 years old. In 1750 the Jews came to Piotrkow because there were lots of opportunities for them at the time. The Polish King gave privileges to Jews but they couldn't live in the area within the wall. There were many wooden houses at the time and one wood synagogue. The Jewish Cemetery was outside of the city.

In the 18th century many things changed and the Jewish section of Piotrkow became bigger and richer. There was a new synagogue and they added cemeteries to the town. It encompassed three acers of land.

The Journey continued! Next, we headed to my dad's home town of Sosnowiec.

Once again I asked for confirmation that my dad, Bernard knew we were coming to see him. A few minutes later I got it! There was a large truck with my dad's name written all over it!! We love you dad. What a surreal feeling to see this truck. I felt your presence at that moment.

At 1:30 p.m. we were heading into my father's home town of Sosnowiec. At this point I said out loud in the van "Dad we are coming to see you in your home town. Please give me confirmation so I am aware that you know we are here to see you and your family. After approximately two minutes I looked out to the right of my window and that is where I saw a huge truck next to us. The truck had the most beautiful words written on the back of it "Bernard" and as we passed it, it had "Bernard and Bernard Transport-Logistic, and in the front it said Bernard." It was the biggest shock ever to see my dad's name in bold red and black font, bigger than I could ever imagine. That certainly was confirmation to every one of my family members. I attempted to capture that picture because the old adage is a picture is worth a thousand words, and how true that is. I felt a sense of love at that point. Throughout the journey I continued to get confirmation that loved ones were with me through feathers, dimes, and lady bugs, but this was the best feeling ever.

We saw where my father and his friends Moris Huppert, Jack Feder, and Ted Pilcowitz went to school. Although the school is no longer there, there was another building in its spot. It was on Ostgogerska 9.

At that point I was ready and excited to start exploring Sosnowiec. Not only was I looking for my dad's school but also his friend Moris Huppert and Jack Feder's school on Ostrogorska 9. Kasha put in the street name only without the number so we were just driving aimlessly for a while. Mom asked some young polish men for directions—how wonderful that she was still fluent in Polish. We got back in the van and found it. Well none of us were surprised to see that the Jewish school the boys went to was not there anymore, but the address confirmed we were in the right spot. We entered the building and saw that there were several offices inside, including a therapist's office. There was a patient sitting outside waiting to be seen, and we asked her if she knew there was a school at this exact spot, but she just shook her head no. Possibly she did not understand English. We asked several other people on the street but no one knew anything about a Jewish boy's school.

Next door at Ostrogorska 7 was Moris Huppert's residence. The doors were locked but we managed to capture a photograph of it. It looked like an old apartment building with lots of mailboxes visible as soon as people enter. It was extremely moving to Moris when he saw our photograph. He asked "How did you find out where I lived?" He had tears in his eyes. What an unbelievable moment for him to go back and see where he lived over 80 years ago. His daughter Rita recalled stories from the past of her father sharing where he lived in Sosnowiec.

As we explored the area we saw some plaques hung up outside of what looked like a school that documented where the Jews were hung to death. We knew we were in the location where the Jewish families lived and went to school. How surreal that once again we are walking in the path where my dad and his family walked. Anne, my sister-in-law continued to point out feathers on our path. She said "Lori here is another feather, your grandparents are with you." Feathers were seen throughout this town and others. I even saw two mezuzahs on some doors. It continued to confirm there was Jewish existence there! The Nazis did their best to extinguish all traces of the Jewish humanity but yet seventy plus years later there are still bits of reminders that life for the Jews did exist.

We saw some plaques and monuments documenting the exact spots where the Nazis hung the Jews and where they were forced to gather in the park (the Jewish ghetto of Srodula).

At this point my mother was anxious to leave and head to Krakow, but we persuaded her to at least find where the Jewish ghetto was in Sosnowiec. Kasha programmed it into the GPS and began driving. As I looked around, I saw a large mall, beautiful modern stores, and once again it was hard to believe we were really here. Who would believe these old towns could be so modern? Kasha arrived at the destination but we were not sure if this was the spot. Mark and Jeff got out to explore a large park. Finally they found the confirmation! In the center of the park was a large square granite with a Jewish star engraved in the center. It documented this was the spot of the Jewish ghetto. This is where the Nazis forced thousands of Jews from the town to stay before they were deported to death camps. Once again, with the park filled with old people sitting on benches and enjoying the serenity, and the youth playing on the swings and running around, did anyone bother to read and look at this most meaningful monument that documented the terror that happened in the 1940's? It is hard to believe how Nazis were so inhumane to loving people. Well Dad, I did not explore your home because mom was ready to go, but your presence was definitely felt here. You will always be in our hearts! I love you forever!

Finally we arrived in the most beautiful and medieval looking city, Krakow. It was not destroyed in WW2 and as a result of this the buildings remained as they were. We walked through the Jewish quarter and the city square.

We headed over to Krakow. What a beautiful city. I can't wait to explore. Last night we arrived in the majestic city of Krakow. We checked into the Ester Hotel last night, and upon entering we heard beautiful Jewish music played by four performers. We were in the Jewish quarters. How amazing once again that Judaism prevails in this section of Krakow. I sat outside with the family for a while and just enjoyed the sites. We walked a few streets to an exciting hub where there were lots of young people eating at outdoor cafes and walking around. I am so excited for tomorrow's adventures.

July 13, 2016 morning
Krakow, Poland—Hotel Ester is located at Ul. Szeroka 20, 31-053 Krakow (http://hotel-ester.krakow.pl)

This was in the heart of the Jewish quarters. As we began exploring, we noticed there was a synagogue a few feet across from us, a Jewish book store, a beauty shop and several delicious Jewish restaurants. Mom treated us to an excursion on a golf cart to the three sections of Krakow. My friends John and Paulette mentioned this was one of the best tours they took. Our guide was one of the only African Americans I saw in all of Poland. He came to Poland to study in school. He took us to the Jewish Quarter first.

Above left: Basilica of the Holy Trinity and Dominican monastery; right: Town Hall Tower in Krakow

In the Jewish Quarter we saw two Jewish cemeteries, synagogues, churches and more. He stated there were 7 synagogues in Krakow, 165 churches, two cultures (Judaism and Christianity) and presently one synagogue is still open and active. This is an Orthodox synagogue. He pointed out the courtyard in front of the synagogue still performs weddings and other ceremonies. At that spot there were 30 Poles that were executed back in the 1920's. Sharoka Street was "The life of the Jewish area."

He stated Helena Rubenstein was born in a house at Max 14, near the Hotel Ester in Krakow's Kazimierz's district. Her Polish name was Chaja Rubenstein born in 1872. She was a business woman, philanthropist, and art collector on top of a cosmetic genius. She was married, had two children, and eventually got divorced and moved to Australia and then ended up in New York.

Our guide told us the story about Issac Synagogue. This was the largest synagogue in Krakow. The clerk was murdered on the Jewish commune by the Nazis because he would not set fire to his synagogue. We also heard the story about the Augustine Church. This was built for the King due to all his sins and adulteress affairs.

There was the Synagogue Temple which was used as stables for horses during the War. It was restored after the war. How despicable that the Nazis used a sacred place to keep horses! Also there was Kuppa Synagogue which means "Treasure." This was around in the 17th century.

Tour 2 began and this was called the Old Time Krakow Tour which covered the market square of the Old Town. It is also called the grand square in Krakow. Now we get to go to the heart of the city where the medieval buildings exist. Here we saw castles, churches, forts, gothic towers of the St. Mary's Basilica Church, and more. The main square of the Old Town of Krakow is the center of the city. This area was built in the 13th century. People were buried in the Royal Castle. The guide shared that the Pope came and spoke from one of the buildings here. He stated the Dominican Church was under construction due to a fire.

Above left: Barbican; right: St. Mary's Basilica and the old Market Square

There was the beautiful looking Barbican structure which had the shape of a saucer. It was built in the 16th century and was a "circular marvel of military architecture." It has seven turrets on the top and 130 loopholes in rows and the lower part was to be used by artillery and the upper part for rifles. It was surrounded by a moat. If enemies came in they would have been trapped by all sides. The guide said summer concerts are held there now.

We rode under the gate of the beautiful Wawel Cathedral. Wawel Cathedral was seen at the end of Kanonicza Street. This street was part of the Royal road. One should definitely go to this street.

At night it is lit up and vendors are there selling their goods. Little sparkly toys were being shot up in the sky, and people were passing through in horse draw carriages. Visitors or natives to Krakow were eating in the lovely outdoor cafes and it was a hopping spot until the square shuts down at 2:00 a.m. Also, we saw the second oldest university in Europe. Nicolaus Copernicus attended there. He was a brilliant astronomer and mathematician. The first oldest university was in Prague. We also saw the oldest theater in Krakow. What a spectacular and wonderful surprise to see this spot!

Tour 3 was the Tour of Oskar Schindler's Factory and more. The tour guide shared there were 68,000 Jews in Krakow—65,000 gone forever—and only 3,000 Jews survived. The Nazis transferred all the Jews to the Jewish ghetto in Krakow. 15,000 people squeezed into 3 ghetto areas. They were deported to Plaszow camp. Originally it was going to be a work camp but due to the shortage of food and horrible conditions it soon became a concentration camp. Most prisoners did not even last four weeks.

The ghetto wall was knocked down in September of 1943. There were many Jews that lived near the Vistula River. They were forced to move across the river. The Jews were allowed to carry a few possessions such as their most essential items and as a result of this many carried chairs. They thought they were moving to a new home. The Nazis set them up in a ghetto in 1941 and they were surrounded by a wall. It was called the "Jewish Residential Area."

We saw the "Empty Chairs Memorial" in Krakow. There were 70 bronze chairs all around Plac Bohaterow Getta. The chairs represent all of the loss as the ghetto was liquidated and all of the prisoners' possessions were thrown on the streets. When one wanders past this spot, one cannot help but wonder why are there chairs mounted to the pavement? What significance does this have to life in Krakow? How deceiving the Nazis were to have them bring their possessions. There was constant lies and deceit and humiliation every step of the way!

Our guide continued to take us in golf carts past "Apteka" which is the Polish word for pharmacy. This pharmacy had the most significance to the Jewish life. This pharmacy called Apteka Pod Orlem became a historical museum. Here was a Gentile man named Tadeusz Paniewicz, a pharmacist who, along with his staff, sacrificed their own well-being to help the Jews. It is so heartwarming to learn that there were the righteous among Poland!

The English transliteration is "Pharmacy under the Eagle." It was located on Pl. Bohaterow Getta. He was the only Polish citizen allowed to stay and work in the ghetto. This Pharmacist assisted with providing food, medicine, falsifying documents for the Jews and helping the Jews to avoid deportation. His staff along with Schindler helped to save 1,100 Jews.

Roman Polansky was one of Schindler's men to survive the war. Later on he produced the movie *The Pianist*. I could not wait to go to Schindler's Factory. Finally after watching the movie (1993) and learning so much about this righteous man, my family and I would finally be approaching those gates. We were told the factory did not change in 50 years. It was kept exactly the same. They did put up a list of photos of the Jews that were rescued. There is also a sign on the wall that says "whoever saves one life saves the entire world." His factory produced pots, bombs, detonators, and more. Tomorrow we will get tickets to go inside and see Schindler's Factory.

After our tour ended we had lunch, and then explored Krakow on our own. Jeff had some Lubavitch boys from Poland stop by his office each week to see if anyone wanted Tefillin. As Jeff became acquainted with them, he shared that he was going to go to Poland. The boys shared that their uncle was a Rabbi at the Chabad house in Krakow. Sure enough, Jeff went walking with us and within a few blocks we saw the Chabad house. He went in inquiring about the Rabbi. He was not there today but we had plans on going to hear the Klezmer band tomorrow evening with hopes of meeting the Rabbi. At times I feel like we are all connected to one another, even in different continents.

"G-d must have been on leave during the Holocaust"

—*Simon Wiesenthal*

4,456 Miles

July 13th, 2016 afternoon in Auschwitz, in Oswiecim

So the dreaded bus tour to Auschwitz begins. To my surprise there was a video shown of authentic clips of prisoners in Auschwitz. I wanted to avert my eyes but kept going back to the video. I felt so awful that Mom had to watch this video. I told her she could close her eyes and take a nap before we arrived. It was still so hard to believe that she along with my family were going to retrace the steps in Auschwitz. In my mind I was thinking who would ever want to go back to the place where they feared for their lives every minute of the day, where there was no food or water, where death emanated all around you. Why put yourself through this misery?

Well in her mind, the answer was simple. She said if she was going to Poland she has to go to Auschwitz to see if she could get answers to what happened to her brother Srulek (Israel). She was hoping to find pictures of him. She was ready to finally say her goodbyes, since that was the last place she saw him. He was in line with Mom and Aunt Felicia before selection. He was told to go to the left and my mother and aunt were going to the right. Tears were shed and that was the last time they saw their young brother. As he walked away he stopped and stared at them and cried. Never to be seen again.

We all thought that was where he perished. To my surprise, while I was in Poland I received an email from the ITS (International Tracing Society) following up on the search Anne initiated and found that he was transported to Bergen-Belsen. How ironic that my mother and aunt were also transported there but none of them knew he was there too. Was he there at the same time as them? The men were transported in all male boxcars while the women were transported in all female boxcars. Why was it that their paths never crossed? I wonder if he would have survived knowing he had family there instead of being all alone.

Prior to coming to Auschwitz I emailed the museum asking for photos of him and asking for documentation on him. They said documents were destroyed prior to liquidation. All documents I came across always said "Presumably dead" while other members of our family said "Dead." So the question lingered did he really die? My mother said after the camps were liberated and they were put in the DP (Displaced Persons) camp the Red Cross was actively searching for survivors but they never could get any information on him. Some brave few went back to their homes but there were stories that the Jews that tried to go back home were shot or killed because there was still so much anti-Semitism there.

I recently heard a 91 year old survivor speak and, when he went back to his home in Hungary, some other people were in his home and would not evacuate. He said he went up to his attic and took out a hidden gun and was ready to use it but by that time the people that were residing there left. He said his sister and brother came back and they were reunited. He believed one other brother perished in the war, but to their surprise a neighbor said they saw him in Germany. The next day they went to the city in Germany and were reunited with him. What a miracle that all the siblings in his family survived. That is extremely rare. Unfortunately my mother (the youngest sibling in her family) and my aunt (who may have been like a mother figure to her) were the only two in their family that survived.

So here we are in Auschwitz. It was a cold, gloomy, miserable day. I was so nervous to enter the grounds with my mother. We saw the infamous wrought iron sign that said "Arbeit Macht Frei" which means "Work Sets you Free." There was never any intention for freedom, but for death to all whether they worked or not. The Nazis goal was to kill everyone as fast as possible and not leave a trace of Jewish life!

From the beginning months of 1942-the late months of 1944 transport trains were sending thousands and thousands of Jews to the gas chambers. In Auschwitz there were more than one million prisoners who died. The majority of these prisoners were Jews, and my family, as well as family of innocent people. There were also Poles that perished here as well as Sinti, Romani, and more.

The rail road tracks were used to transport millions of Jews in cattle cars.

Many were killed in crematoriums within the first 20 minutes of their arrival. The others suffered from starvation, disease, executions, medical experiments, and even suicide. Who could tolerate such extreme torture?

4,456 Miles

I can hear Mom crying the words "Why, Why" at her mother's grave site. The answer is that there is such extreme hatred for other religions! Will history ever learn from these horrific acts of prejudice? I would like to say yes but when you see genocide still occurring in all different parts of the world you think no, they have not learned. My mother was excited that over 1.7 million people come each year to Auschwitz to learn about these atrocities. So maybe one day people will learn to embrace other religions and differences in the world.

What was shocking to me was when the Red Cross would come in to observe, the Nazis set up one part of the camp to look like the prisoners were playing soccer and others were playing instruments in an orchestra. What deceit!

My parents both miraculously survived Auschwitz. The German sign "Arbeit Macht Frie" meant "Work sets you free" but in reality, the Nazis mission was to kill all the Jews and anyone else who was not Aryan.

Upon entering the grounds my mother was shocked by the landscape. There was grass! There were trees. "If only there was grass and trees then, we would have eaten it." The infamous sign was partially camouflaged by a large beautiful tree. Many bunkers were gone! It was large but almost vacant. I personally had the feeling that I was entering a college campus with many dorms until I walked into a bunker. Oh was I wrong. What was inside took my breath away.

These were the bunkers that people slept in. There was only wood bunkers inside and several people had to share one spot to sleep. There were no blankets or pillows. Mom and Felicia were in bunker 26. On Mom's return to Auschwitz her plan is to step foot in Bunker 26. What an unbelievably brave woman!

It was dark, stark, and shocking. There was a huge room with glass windows portraying 30,000 pairs of thin, worn out shoes that the prisoners wore. It was a huge amount, but can you imagine if they had all the shoes for over 1 million prisoners. The next glass display had hair filled to the capacity. Each prisoner was shaven of his/her hair. I thought to dehumanize them. Little did I know that the Nazis used the hair for seat cushions and upholstery. The hair was pressed into felt. It was also used for lining boots for the troops as well as spun into yarn for socks. It was also used by the guards to protect them from lice which carried typhus. Another window was filled with prosthetics, such as prosthetic legs. There were hundreds of these crammed into the room.

They even removed gold from the prisoner's teeth. How disgusting and barbaric. Tattoos were painfully put on the prisoner's arms and chest. Now they were merely a number. My father had a number and when my brother and I were young and asked him about his number, he did not want to instill the terror, fear, and hatred in us so he merely stated it was his phone number. My mother and aunt were fortunate that the Nazis had so many prisoners arriving each day that they could not keep up with tattooing everyone.

There was a large mural of prisoners on the wall inside the museum. My friend Paula who works for the FIDF said when she was in Auschwitz in June 2016 there was a survivor with her. She recognized herself in the painting. How unbelievable was that? There were many photos of prisoners on the wall with their names. I stopped to read each and every one of these in the first part of the tour, but unfortunately Mom's missing brother Srulek was not on the wall. How she had hoped to get a picture of him. That would have meant the world to her!

We also saw thin, worn out, flimsy, and dirty looking blankets where maybe ten prisoners slept in one small area. Another bunker had hay on the floor. When it rained it was wet and cold. It is so unimaginable to see these conditions. There was a wall where prisoners were taken to be executed. There was also a crematorium where the prisoners were first poisoned then burned.

How were Mom and Aunt Felicia so lucky to survive? I was told one out of every two prisoners were killed.

There was a small room where prisoners were punished by having to stand with several other prisoners until they died. They were starved to death. Can you imagine no food or water and just waiting to die?

If you were lucky you received one piece of bread and one bowl of watered down soup to be passed from prisoner to prisoner. I read sometimes the Nazis would put nails, needles, or other items in the soup. Wow, how fortunate for a prisoner to find a weapon like that? I hoped they were used as a weapon on the Nazi guards.

After a while my mother had enough! We sat outside for a while waiting to catch up with the rest of the family. I kept offering to go to the bus and stop observing this torture.

We observed tour groups from all over the world: Spain, Israel, families with young children and older people. The world continued to have an interest! We were wondering if it was fair to charge money to get in, charge money to use the rest rooms, and have a little shop with books. I thought it was awful for them to profit from others' tragedies. I do understand it is a museum and money is needed to keep up the grounds and to hire docents and staff to run it. It just infuriates me that money is pouring in!

Now that we are thoroughly depressed and drained we had to get back on the bus and ride three kilometers (1.8 miles) to the

Next we went to Birkenau which was three kilometers (less than two miles) from Auschwitz. No one survived here.

4,456 Miles

connecting death camp: Birkenau. Now this did not look like a museum. This was a dramatic change from Auschwitz. Here we saw large railroad tracks that stretched for what looked like an eternity entering into the enormous death camp. It was the largest of the death camps and it could hold up to 150,000 prisoners at a time. Here we saw many crematoriums, barbed wire, light houses where guards observed and randomly shot prisoners, and many bunkers. Inside the crematorium was dark and frightening. I could imagine the lines of prisoners walking in, getting poisoned, screaming due to the pain, and then all that was left were ashes. Then the next group did the same.

It went on and on until they could not keep up and the machine stopped functioning for the day. There was one crematorium in rubble that was destroyed by the Nazis so that there would be no evidence left.

The crematorium where they poisoned the prisoners and burned them to ashes. The Germans burned these down before liberation so there would be no evidence left!

I was told prisoners had jobs such as digging enormous ditches and another shift of prisoners would come in and dump bodies in there and cover it with dirt. The whole process was repeated day after day after day.

Prisoners were beaten or shot because of normal bodily functions such as sneezing or coughing. The shocking thing was the guards would go home and then eat dinner, play with their children, help with homework, tuck their children into bed, etc. and have a normal life. This was hard to comprehend. Didn't they have an ounce of compassion? Was there not one thread of decency in their body? Were they really human or merely robots taking orders?

So the journey back on the bus to Krakow was silent. You could hear a pin drop. People were depressed, drained, shocked, and speechless.

Mom survived this visit back! She did not get any more answers about her brother but she was able to say goodbye. I was disappointed that I did not get any confirmation that he was there. When I told Jeff that night that I was so disappointed that there was no confirmation from my Uncle Srulek (Israel), Jeff said to me "I did not want to mention this earlier, but when I went to the restroom with your Mom, there was a butterfly circling over our heads." How unbelievable was that. There were no flowers there, no nectar for them to eat, yet there was one beautiful butterfly in such a horrific, gloomy, desolate place, and that butterfly was circling over their heads! Maybe that was the sign my mother needed. It gave me a little comfort!

On a positive note the Rabbi and the young professionals from New York's J. Roots Journey sent us the following photos:

My family with all of them at the synagogue in Piotrkov.

All the young adults and Rabbi visiting our grandmother's grave site in The Lodz Cemetery. They said prayers to lift her soul! We were all so touched by this loving act of kindness.

July 14, 2016—Krakow

The beautiful plaque on the wall in memory of Miriam Ferber's husband's family. Mom plays canasta sometimes with Miriam.

In the morning Mom and I went to the synagogue in the Jewish Quarter and we saw a beautiful plaque on the wall in memory of Miriam Ferber's husband's family. Once again the world seems so connected to us, as my mother plays Canasta sometimes with Miriam. The plaque stated "Thou shall not kill" In loving memory of the Ferber Family.

This is a cemetery in Krakow. It is very old but the tombstones are kept up.

Next we explored the Jewish Cemetery which was connected to the Synagogue. I asked a young man with a yarmulke where he was from. He said he was from New York and I told him I was from outside of Detroit. He said wait here and he brought two others

4,456 Miles

from Detroit to join us. One was Rabbi Burman. What a small world that Rabbi Burman runs Partners in Torah where my friend Alex attends. Alex and others travel with Rabbi Burman to Israel and all over the world. Partners in Torah is located in Southfield where Jeff grew up. Once again I am interwoven with Poland and my life back home!

We explored the Jewish Cemetery and met two others from Detroit—one was Rabbi Burman and the woman was Andrea Lederman.

The Rabbi asked Mom to share what she remembered most about being in Auschwitz. I believe she said the chaos and fear of being there. They could not believe she was a survivor and was able to make this trip. He too brought a whole group of young professionals with him to Poland and Prague. Once again, it was comforting to Mom to know thousands of people, Jews and non-Jews come to Poland to be educated on the Holocaust.

Jeff and Lori Ellis, Anne and Mark Klisman and Sophie Tajch Klisman standing at the gate of Schindler's Factory.

133

In the afternoon we went to Schindler's Factory. Oskar Schindler was a hero as he saved over one thousand Jews from death by having them work in his factory protecting them, giving them food, drink, and medicine. It was surreal to stand by Oskar Schindler's entrance, the famous gate. It was very moving to see photos of the 1,100 Jews he saved all over the wall of his factory.

Above are photos at Schindler's Factory of the 1,100 Jews he rescued and a photo of Oskar Schindler seen on the wall behind his office. He was a righteous Pole and when he died his body was buried in Israel. If you have not seen the movie **Schindler's List** *it would be worth your time to view it!*

I walked in Schindler's office where he met with his accountant and that is where they had meetings on how to save the Jews. I was told prior to the war he was a womanizer and not very honest. He made a total transformation when the war broke out and had a different outlook on life, how to help the Jews.

As we continued with the tour of Schindler's Factory I soon discovered most of this museum was not about Oskar Schindler but rather the Jews in Poland. I soon learned that during the German occupation Poland was to be "Germanized." There were 30 prisons and then Germany started renaming the towns and streets into German sounding names. Lodz ghetto became Litzmannstadt ghetto, and more.

4,456 Miles

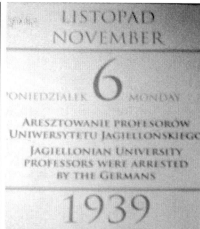

Above left: When The Nazis invaded Poland they Germanized the town by changing street names, changing the town's names and more. Lodz became Litzmannstadt. These signs portrays this change.
Above right: This sign states "Professors were arrested by the Germans." Jews were not allowed to attend University or any school.

In Prashu Concentration Camp in 1932 there were both Jews and Poles there. In September 1943–July 1944 there were 4,000 executed and 80,000 died. There were only 8,000 prisoners left.

The swastika used to be a positive ancient religious symbol and was seen in Buddhism, Hinduism as well as Jainism. My son, Joshua, said he frequently saw the swastika when he traveled to India. It meant luck. Hitler used the symbol with the Nazis in WWII and made it notorious.

The Germans spread propaganda about the Jews and said they had lice and typhus. They were not allowed to continue their education. There was a photo of a sign that stated professors were arrested by the Germans. My mother was forced to stop her education after being in Lodz for only a few years. With strong determination she continued her education upon her liberation in Germany and in the United States.

I learned the swastika used to be a positive symbol and was used in India and several other countries until Hitler used the symbol and made it notorious.

Lori Klisman Ellis

Toys were created to be demeaning to the Jews.

The museum attempted to replicate the Jewish ghetto. Tombstones were broken up and used to create walls in the ghetto. Next we walked through the replica of a concentration camp. This was an eerie feeling as the museum combined auditory with visuals. Not only did we feel the uneven pavement when we entered the replica of the camp, but we saw a bunker, the barbed wire, a safe house and we heard loud dogs barking and the trains in the background. My mother said this was a much more authentic experience than at Auschwitz.

The museum attempted to replicate the Jewish ghetto. Tombstones were broken up and used to create walls in the ghetto. It was so painful to hear these stories and know my loving parents and all the Jews in Europe endured unimaginable suffering!

The museum stated they want to eventually add another sense, olfactory. They want to have the smell of chicken soup permeate through some of the rooms in the museum. It was painful to hear all these stories and know my loving parents endured unimaginable suffering. Once again my mother showed such courage and strength as she listened to the docent go over these stories of the Jews in Poland. Every tour and every excursion was a painful reminder of the past.

In the evening we wanted to end on a positive note so we went to the Chabad house and listened to a Klezmer concert. The music brought back memories of my Dad and Mom—they loved these songs and so do I. It was a talented group of men, who surprisingly were not Jewish but demonstrated an expertise in their music. It was so soothing and peaceful. We needed this to be able to see some beauty in Poland.
To my surprise I saw a bright light or aura there which signifies a loved one who passed is with us in spirit. I felt my father and grandparents presence with all of us during that uplifting and magical evening.

We had to end the evening on a more uplifting note, so we went to the Klezmer concert at the Chabad house. Klezmer music is a musical tradition of the Ashkenazi Jews. It is all instrumental and no lyrics. Initially we were the only ones there but slowly it filled up. We all loved the music. The talent was amazing. There was the most talented viola player, an organ player, a drummer—he did not have the typical set of drums but rather it looked like a wash board, and a cello player. Together they sounded amazing. They played traditional Jewish music. I remember hearing several of these songs at home, and it brought back beautiful memories of my father. By the way, Jeff was happy to finally meet the Rabbi from Krakow. Once again, what a small world.

When we arrived home we shared our visit to Schindler's factory with my parents' friend, Moris Huppert. Moris said he saved Oskar's life. He told us when the camps were liquidated, the

Nazis were being hunted down and prosecuted. Moris said that Oskar tracked down Moris in a Displaced Person's camp and made him (along with others) sign a document that stated that Oskar had saved the lives of Jews and did not kill them. This document would allow Oskar to be free. He was known as the Righteous. After the war Oskar became broke and the Jews were there for him. He was one of the non-Jews to be buried in Israel! The old adage is true, pay it forward.

Now I am looking forward to tomorrow's trip to the mountains in Zakopane. When Mom was a little girl she always heard of this place but never ever imagined she would go. So we hired a private tour to take us in the mountains!

July 15, 2016—Our day in Zakopane

And so her dreams of going to Zakopane high up in the Tatra Mountains came to fruition! Left: Sophie Klisman and her son Mark Klisman. Right: Lori and Jeff Ellis at Tatra Mountain.

And so Mom's dreams of going to Zakopane high up in the Tatra Mountains came to fruition. Zakopane is located in the south of Poland. It is in the southern part of Podhale region. It borders Slovakia. It is approximately 800–1,000 meters above sea level. It took us approximately two hours to get to Zakopane from Krakow. There is a population of close to 30,000 people living there. It is a popular tourist spot for skiing, snowboarding, ski jumping, training for the Olympics, hiking, and more. It gets two and a half million visitors a year there.

When we arrived we saw beautiful chalets nestled into the mountains. There was a bustling down town filled with ski shops, clothing stores, restaurants, and tons of people.

As a young girl my mother heard stories of how beautiful this resort was. Who would ever have thought she would be the one to survive? Who thought she would come back to Poland, and 87 years later she would go back to her roots and see the famous and beautiful Zakopane. Thank goodness she was up for this challenging adventure.

I booked a private one day tour through Viator, to take us to Zakopane. I wanted to end on a positive experience and for one day not think about the horrific events of the war. Our driver, who actually seemed like a race car driver, drove us through the winding, uphill roads.

On the way there we stopped in a small town just a couple miles away from Zakopane where we got out of the car and walked into

4,456 Miles

a wooden house that was actually a store. There was an elderly gentleman selling his large wooden statues of Mary, wooden crosses, and much more. We walked the streets for a while admiring the wooden homes. He shared with us that there was a law that the homes had to be washed on the outside with soap and water once a year, in order to maintain the clean and beautiful appearance.

We bought cheese from the young polish girls outside. It was a smoked cheese made from goat's milk. It looked like loaves of bread and corn on the cob. Next we mingled with a polish woman selling her goods.

When we arrived a few minutes later to Zakopane we saw beautiful chalets nestled into the mountains. There was a bustling downtown filled with ski shops, clothing stores, restaurants, and tons of people. The one street with the most stores is called Krupowki. It had a charming feel to it. You could pick up souvenirs as well as beautiful ski clothes. We bought cheese from the young Polish girls outside. It was a smoked cheese made from goat's milk. It looked like loaves of bread and corn on the cob. Next we mingled with a typical Polish women wearing the traditional babushka. She was selling her goods.

We went on a ski lift high up in the mountains. What a spectacular view! We climbed several steps in the mountain until we reached the highest point. That is where I was mesmerized by

We went on a ski lift high up in the mountains. What a spectacular view. Mom decided to sit this one out.

the mountainous area. My mother observed and choose not to participate in this activity.

So after seeing this beautiful town of Zakopane it is hard to believe there is such wealth there, while some of the other cities have such poverty. Also, it was not destroyed in WWII while Warsaw was brought down to rubble. What a hidden treasure!

And now our journey is coming to an end. On the ride back Anne asked if we could pass through Slovakia. So for twenty minutes we were in another country. It looked just like Poland. It was interesting to me that we just drove through the country without being stopped

Next the driver took us to a lovely chapel and to a near-by town with all homes made up of log cabins.

He took us through another country, Slovakia which looked like Poland.

and asked for our passports. We made the long drive back to Warsaw since we were flying home the next day.

As I reflected on the past ten days of this journey I felt such mixed emotions. I got a totally different perspective of all the lessons I read about and heard by experiencing it through my mother's eyes as well as being here and seeing it for myself. It still boggles my mind how such atrocities happened to innocent, loving people. I hope it brought some closure to my mother. Jeff, Mark, Anne, and I feel so blessed to have had this opportunity to come to Poland! Mom was thrilled that many different nationalities came here to get educated about the atrocities that occurred, so history will not repeat itself.

July 16, 2016—Homeward bound.

And so the journey ends, I thought. There was an incident at the LOT Polish Airport with me. Mark, Anne, Mom, Jeff and I had our boarding passes and were ready to go past security. Well everyone's boarding passes scanned and the doors opened except for mine. There was not a barcode on my boarding pass. A loud buzzer sounded and a large red X appeared on the computer. The door would not open and it would not allow me to leave. The security personnel indicated I had to go back to the polish airlines desk and get a new boarding pass.

I ran over there and saw a very long line. I did get a new boarding pass with a barcode on it this time! Thank goodness. I met up with my family and thought I was in the clear now. We shopped for a few souvenirs in the airport and wasted time until we were ready to board the plane. Everyone in my family went through the boarding process but once again my new boarding pass emitted a bright red X and a loud buzzer. I said to myself, someone does not want me to leave Poland!

I was told to go to the Transfer Desk and get security to approve me and search my luggage. I could hear Mom yell "she is my daughter!" Security stated they would hold the plane for me. Thank goodness I would not have to miss this flight. I made it to the desk and the female security agent patted me down and used the wand, and also searched my luggage. I was grateful I did not have any suspicious items on me. I wonder why I was targeted. I guess I would not be stuck in Poland forever after all. I made it to the plane and Mark said he was going to start a campaign to "Get Lori out of Poland." I appreciated his humor at that point. Now for the long flight to Chicago and back to Michigan. It was approximately 11 hours and 4,456 miles to get home.

When we landed I thought of what my friend Paulette said after her travels. She wants to kiss the ground every time she comes back safe and sound. We made it safely. What an unbelievable journey we had. I wondered what I would do now so I would never forget this experience. And so I began thinking that it took 77 years to get to this point and 4,456 miles to get some closure.

Some of the differences in Poland vs USA

Poland is predominately Catholic. I saw one African American, 0 Muslims, 0 Chaldeans, and a small amount of Jews.

There are tons of beautiful churches and only a handful of synagogues.

There are not many expressways. Therefore, what should take 2–2½ hours to travel can take 5 plus hours.

Water must be purchased at a restaurant. When I bought 2 large bottles of water I spent 39 zloty which is equivalent to approximately $9.00 It was cheaper to buy wine and beer. Maybe that is why Fetal Alcohol Syndrome is so prevalent in Poland.

I feel lucky to be living in the USA!!

Chapter 17 Mediums & Spiritual Posts

I have always been fascinated with mediums and people like Rebecca Rosen. While I was in Poland I asked for some confirmation that my grandparents, uncles, and father knew we were there and could feel our presence. Each day something happened.

It started when I opened my suitcase to pack for the trip and found a dime in the luggage, which signifies a grandparent is watching over me. When in Warsaw's ghetto a white feather fell on my shoe and each day I have found feathers on the ground, especially all over Dad's home town of Sosnowiec. Another day I found two coins on the seat in our van. Anne said Aunt Felicia and Uncle Roman were sitting with us in the van, so I better not sit on them! When I woke up in the morning there was a dime on my luggage. I asked Jeff if he put it there and he said no! When we were at the Polin Museum I saw 8 ladybugs. When we went to the cemetery for my grandmother there were butterflies flying over my head. When in Auschwitz Jeff and Mom went to the restroom and he said there was a butterfly flying over their heads. There are no flowers there so one typically does not see any butterflies.

As I mentioned in an earlier post, when I headed to Dad's hometown in Sosnowiec I asked for confirmation that he knew we were there, to see his house and schools. A big truck drove next to me that said "Bernard and Bernard Logistics" in huge letters all over the truck. Also, Mark had guardian angels surrounding him at the restaurant in Lodz. I felt comforted by all these signs, even if Mom thinks I am a bit crazy!

August 17, 2016—Mediums & Spiritual Posts

"All spiritual practices is the art of shifting perspectives."
—Teal

After my Poland trip I decided to meet with Lynn Darmon, a medium, to follow up on my spiritual feelings from the trip. I had a half an hour appointment and I got subtle messages from her that were accurate and other times it depended on how I interpreted her reading. It went as follows:

As she walked me in the first thing she said to me was "your father's presence is with you now." He passed within a few years but he had health issues (not one, but many over the last 7–8 years). He was a soft and compassionate man. She said he had a kind soul. He was a hard worker. Lynn mentioned he had a good sense of humor even though he was quiet. He never complained. He never wanted anyone to worry about him. She said when he passed he had trouble breathing. He wanted us to know he is fine now. He does not have trouble breathing now. She asked if he had trouble with his gait when he was ill. I said yes, he was non-ambulatory at the end. She also said there were a lot of health issues not just the breathing and walking.

"He was a business man." She saw numbers around him (numbers on his arm or money?). She said he had his own business. He was under 6 feet tall (he was approximately 5'9" and a very neat, slender and handsome man).

He is with his two brothers on the other side. They are reunited now. She said they were separated but back together. Lynn said the two brothers were closer, possibly due to being close in age. (My dad was the younger brother and was in Sosnowiec at the time the war broke out, while his two older brothers left Poland because the conditions were getting bad and went to Russia. One was sent to a prison there. After the war they were sent to Australia while my dad was sent to the USA.)

Lynn said my dad was separated from his brothers for a lifetime (they were separated in the Holocaust). She said one brother is Jakob! He is also with a younger male with the initial "M" (possibly it is my Uncle Moszek, which was Mom's older brother).

She also mentioned he is with a Roz (my grandmother's name was Rozrawaska). She did not think it was her because typically a mother-in-law would be older, but she was not older. (She passed away at a young age of 51 due to the conditions in the ghetto.) Lynn also said "Your dad is with someone with the initial "E" possibly Ester" (Mom had a sister that passed away before she was born named "Esteria"). She said both of Mom's sisters are stepping forward (possibly Esteria and Aunt Felicia).

Lynn said my Dad kept pointing to his pocket and asked if he kept his glasses there or pens. She saw a clip which was used to hold his glasses in place. She said this was his confirmation to let me know it was him. She said he is pointing to his wrist, as if we have a watch of his. Josh and Aaron kept one of his many watches. He saved all his watches whether they worked or not.

Lynn stated there was a recent event that took place 6-8 months ago and he was with us. I could not confirm this, and then she said a recent event will take place in 6-8 months and he will be with our family. She sees red roses. He is celebrating the family outcome.

Lynn said I have two kids, a son and daughter. They feel great and are independent. One got a new job a few months ago. He is watching over them and me. He saw that one traveled a lot (possibly Josh as he went to India).

Lynn sees me with red roses. She said I had a birthday in the spring, March or April, and he was celebrating with me. She said he is still celebrating his birthdate in December. She wanted me to know if I see coins or feathers to think of him. That is his message to me. (Well I did find the dime when I began packing, and feathers were dropping on my shoes, and all over the ground in Poland.)

Lynn mentioned I am in a transition phase, but doing well. Prior to coming to this meeting, I asked for my Dad's presence to be felt, my Aunt Felicia, my old friend Marilyn (a colleague from Royal Oak Schools, whom I wrote *Laughing While Learning, All Kidding Aside)*, and any others who wanted to communicate with me.

During the reading, someone was poking through, first quietly then louder and louder. She said Marilyn kept saying her name out loud and wanted to make sure I knew she was OK. She was playing cards at a table or playing Mahjong. She was seen with three kids; however she just had one son, Mathew who passed away prior to her passing. She said she is feeling great. She was a fun loving person. She loved the outdoors. She had a birthday in October (however her birthday was in February).

So I had mixed feelings when I left that session. Did my Dad feel our presence in Poland? That was never mentioned. The truck with the blatant message of "Bernard" written on it was never brought up. Could he be with my grandmother (Roz or Rozrazwska)? Who knows? The bottom line is I hope that he is in peace now and no longer suffering from the devastating illness of Alzheimer's disease.

Is there life after death? Coincidentally, I just watched Dr. Oz the other day and there was an episode about life after death. One person was in Hell and back, and another two were in heaven and back. Dr. Oz asked how they came back from the dead. One man answered his wife prayed out loud for his health and safe return from his coma, and an old hand came and pulled him through something that looked like a black garbage bag until he got to the other side. He said he heard beautiful music, like an orchestra and a bright white light, and then he came back to the life he was familiar with.

Several people he interviewed said in heaven it was so beautiful and when people spoke to them it was not through words but they could hear or interpret the messages. A woman on the show said the person that was speaking to her had blue piercing eyes that emitted a glow that was so intense and beautiful. The woman on the Dr. Oz show had a drowning experience from scuba diving and was without oxygen for 10 minutes. Dr. Oz said it only takes 5 minutes for someone to be without oxygen to declare them dead.

Each person that went through this experience stated they did not fear death, but welcomed it when it was their time. Dr. Oz asked how the one man went to Hell when he was shot. I used to believe if you were good in life you would go to Heaven and if you were a terrible person you would go to Hell. This man said the reason he believes he went to Hell was that he did not believe in the Lord. He now believes, and as a result of this does not fear death.

I do believe there can be life after death, but I am not sure what it will be. This reminds me of a book I read years ago, called *Many Lives Many Masters* by Dr. Brain Weiss. The psychiatrist hypnotized his patients and realized they were reincarnated from a previous life. The patients gave such specific details of another world or living during WWI that the Psychiatrist was convinced there was no way of knowing this unless that person actually lived in that era. He also said, even if you are a male now, you could have been a female in a previous life. Some of the people we are surrounded by today may have been in our previous life, although the names have changed, and the gender may have changed. That is why when you meet some people you have that instant connection. It is as if you knew each other for years.

I would like to study the Kabbalah and learn more on that topic. Is there some validity to this? Just because we do not see things does that mean they do not exist?

August 19, 2016 — Meditation

As I was reflecting on my reading by the medium Lynn Darmon from August 17th, I began thinking the three people I asked to hear from: My dad, my Aunt and my old friend Marilyn, and I actually heard from all three. So was there any validity to making an out loud request for confirmation from a family member? I started wondering this before I went to bed. So in the evening before I fell asleep I said out loud "I do not know if I believe in getting messages from the after-life, but if it is possible please let me know where you are Uncle Israel."

I could not fall asleep in my room so I went into Michelle's spare bedroom where I immediately fell asleep. In the middle of the night I must have turned and felt a sharp item against my skin. I thought it may be a pin sticking out of the mattress. With my eyes still closed, in the middle of the night, I yanked at it and pulled something out, and gently placed it on the side table next to her bed.

I proceeded to fall back asleep and hoped to wake up before my 8:00 fusion class at the JCC. When I woke up at 7:20 I had a clear visualization of where Israel was. I saw in color several brownish-red bricks piled up high, standing upright and on the top was an eternal flame. This is where he was buried. Where is this location? Was he buried in one of the concentration camps?

I began searching the internet on topics such as concentration camp monuments with eternal flames. To my surprise I found many of them had flames but not in the shape of an oval standing upright. So I still do not know where he is. As I continued searching I came to the realization that we may never find out this information. I left Lynn a voice message to see if she would have insight on this. It sounds peculiar to ask her psychic abilities but when I read about her online she stated she had found a missing child. When she returned my call she said she would give it some thought and let me know if she comes up with an answer. Unfortunately, she did not! Who knows I may try for confirmation on this again. It was very strange that this was the first thought when I woke up.

The other really unusual thing was that sharp item that was sticking out of Michelle's bed was not a pin, but was a feather. It must be a feather bed and the bottom of the feather was protruding on top of her mattress and that is why I felt a sharp prick. That beautiful white feather also gave me comfort knowing that my dad or possibly Uncle Israel was with me now in spirit and heard my request.

One Last Medium Experience: October, 2017

As a fun gift for my girlfriend's birthday I decided to surprise her with a reading from Elaine Grohman, a spiritual healer. Elaine did a group reading. At times she was on target with some people and then not accurate with others. When she read my sister-in-law, Anne, she said there is someone with the initial B standing by you. It is Bernie or Bernard. Bernard of course is her father-in-law, and my father. He is standing by someone with the initial M, Martin. Martin happened to be my parents close friend who had passed away.

Elaine stated I just went to Israel, but in fact it was Poland. She said I was praying in Hebrew (which was accurate since my family and I put up a tombstone for my mother's family). She said "I see a monument shaped this tall." She extended her hand to the height of her hips. She said "It is curved and someone is rocking by it" (we rock or bow our heads during the prayer). Elaine said our family members who passed said "Thank you for putting up the monument. " She said "There are lots of names on it, not just one." "Your father was there (in spirit) with your mom." "Spirits were with you there."

Next Elaine mentioned that I am writing a journal (which is actually this book)! She described a symbol that needed to be on the cover of the book which is a Chai. She told me to "Finish the book by November and get it in people's hands." She asked if the book is about someone's life. It is mainly about my parents and their family's life in Poland.

Elaine stated my dad was not a bitter person even though he was in the Holocaust. "He had a dry, funny sense of humor." "Uncle Roman was there as well smoking a cigar by the monument. He is here during our gathering and says hello."

She asked if I have any questions and I said "Where is Srulek Israel?" She said he died in Bergen-Belsen. She told me Srulek had a mole or scar by the side of his forehead. She asked if Srulek was 15 years older than Mom. (He was 12 years older than her. He was born in 1917 and Mom was born in 1929). She then asked if I had a relative with an "H name (I am not aware of one).

She told me my dad made things out of wood (he actually finished the basement using wood and made a beautiful bar out of wood). She asked if he made a menorah for me. I said no. She told me I may find a picture of dad with a wooden item. Elaine mentioned my dad had heart issues (he had a pacemaker for years). She said my dad was crazy about me and loved me greatly. She mentioned that my dad would call me "Girly" (which I do not believe to be accurate). Elaine ended by saying the Chai or symbol of life needs to be put on the cover of the book!

A colleague of mine from West Bloomfield School District, Carol shared with me that she gets sent messages from those that have passed on and the messages are on monarchs.

> *"Your parents are a symbol of hope and the metamorphosis alone is symbolic to me. We change from a shell of a physical being (caterpillar) to a chrysalis (Limbo—transition from this world) to a magnificent and beautiful creature with wings to soar to the heavens (butterfly)."*
>
> *"Without hope we have nothing. In the most dreadful physical, mental and spiritual conditions, man can many times survive with hope and prayer with G-d taking over the tasks that we cannot do."*
>
> ~ **Carol Carnley**

Part VII:
Life After The Journey

Chapter 18 Life After The Journey To Poland

*"You can't start the next chapter
if you keep re-reading the last one."*

Provincial

Upon returning to this wonderful place called USA, it is hard to put aside my thoughts on Poland and all the suffering that occurred to millions of innocent people. It must be even harder for my mother to close down those haunting thoughts and get back into her normal life. She always told me that was a different lifetime.

I wonder how she along with all the other survivors were able to assimilate to a new life without having psychiatrists or psychologists available to help them. How could she still believe in G-d? Would they carry hatred and resentment with them forever? How were they able to get married, have children, and not share their prior life with their children? Many did not want their children to know about the atrocities they went through or the hatred that was cast upon them because they were Jewish. How is it possible to still have love and kindness?

When my son, Joshua had his Bar Mitzvah, his Torah portion covered this topic. Rabbi Harold Kushner had a book and video called *When Bad Things Happen to Good People*. It was not why but when. My question to G-d has always been if you are the all mighty G-d how can you not intervene when you witness millions of innocent lives being killed. I was told the answer was that you teach us lessons and then you hope we learned those lessons. You sit back and just observe. That sounds cruel and unfair. The book addressed several topics including the Rabbi's son's illness. It was fascinating to read and interesting to get his perspective on things.

My husband Jeff feels every Jew needs to go to Poland and learn more about the Holocaust. He always felt he had a lot of knowledge about the Holocaust, but when he went to Poland he learned a vast amount about life for Jews during the ghetto and the concentration camps.

Rabbi Shmuel Lynn from New York was on a mission called J. Roots. The Rabbi stated every Jew should experience Poland along with Israel, as part of a new Birthright Trip. I agree this would be a poignant and meaningful journey for young and old Jews alike.

I encourage everyone to experience a journey to Poland, speak to survivors, listen to their stories at the Holocaust Memorial Center, read books on it, and continue to educate yourself and others on this topic. I was excited to hear that the Senate approved Genocide education in schools in Michigan along with several other states. Genocide training can cover the Holocaust along with other places such as Rwanda, Armenian genocide, Cambodian genocide, Bosnian genocide, and unfortunately the list goes on and on.

In the past, teachers had only a page or two in text books that covered these topics. Now classes are available for teachers at the Holocaust Memorial Center that help teach this topic and they can get a curriculum to go along with it. There are matrixes available online for staff to use as a guide when deciding how to introduce this topic, at what age and how to incorporate into social studies, language arts, the arts, research/thinking and ethnics/responsibilities. Refer to a Teacher's Guide on the Holocaust or check with your local Holocaust Memorial Center.

Chapter 19 A Speaker At The Holocaust Center

*"Education and Remembrance are the
only cures for hatred and bigotry."*
—Miriam Oster

Being a speaker at the Holocaust was something my Aunt Felicia had done for years. That was not something my mother ever envisioned doing. After her close friend, Sue Weiss passed away, as well as the passing of my father, my mother felt her life story was never told. Her friends, which were survivors were all getting up there in the years and if they did not tell their story now who would know about it? Some of her friends were fortunate enough to have been photographed and interviewed by Monni Must and her colleagues. My mother and father were portrayed in the trilogy called *Living Witnesses Faces of the Holocaust*. This is a wonderful book about Holocaust survivors.

*"It captures the survivors' personalities and
honors who they were before the war, vividly
depicting their experiences during the war, and
honoring who they became afterward."*
—Monni Must 2013

Others are in *Portraits of Honor*. This was a project created by Dr. Charles Silow, a well-known Psychologist in the area that has dedicated his life's work with survivors. *The Portraits of Honor* can be viewed online at www.portraitsofhonor.org or by going to the Holocaust Memorial Center in Farmington Hills, Michigan. This is an interactive online program that was developed in 1999. This program documents the lives of survivors who live in Michigan. There are photos and biographies on them. Dr. Silow said when you look at their faces you will see "Beauty, resilience and triumph." The C.H.A.I.M group has dedicated their time on working on this project as well.

Others have been interviewed and videotaped for the Shoah Foundation by Steven Spielberg's team. My mother did a different interview and it can be viewed at the Holocaust Memorial Center. Also a copy of her testimony is included in book 2: *Ellis/Klisman Family Tree*.

Now that my sister-in-law, Anne had retired as a counselor for the deaf from Bloomfield Schools, she was interested in becoming a docent at the Detroit Public Library. My mother thought it would be wonderful to have her work as a docent at the Holocaust Memorial Center. Anne decided if she was going to be a docent, my mother should be a speaker, and so the team effort evolved.

Anne was trained by Gail Gruskin Fisher from the Holocaust Memorial Center. She did 6 months of research, passed her exam and became a docent. My mother agreed to speak to 30 students on her first day. That morning my mother received a phone call—instead of speaking to 30 students there would now be 130 students. Anne gave her the option of backing out but my mother always wanted to be a teacher and this would give her the opportunity to educate students. She agreed and did a wonderful job!

Several times a month during the school year my mother speaks to young students from all different ethnic backgrounds. Her oral testimony is included in this book for everyone to read. She recounts events in her life in a chronological order. She speaks about her life in a loving Jewish home with family and friends, then life in the ghetto, life in three concentration camps, life in D.P camps and her journey to America. Her mantra of hope, and not having prejudice is portrayed beautifully in her speech. Her words are so riveting that one can hear a pin drop in the large auditorium at the Holocaust Memorial Center.

My mother shows true empathy for others when she sees her audience crying. She apologizes for making them feel sad. She never wanted pity from others. In reality we do not pity her but have the highest of admiration towards this brave, strong, educated, articulate and beautiful woman. She is a true survivor. She has shown strength for whatever punches life has to throw, and believe me there were many along the way including my father's battle with Alzheimer. She never complained. She showed true compassion and strength along with respect during his care.

Lori Klisman Ellis

Sophie Klisman/Zosia/Zysla Tajch, center was the speaker at the Holocaust Memorial Center in Farmington Hills, Mi. 2018

Additional children at the Holocaust Memorial Center listening to my mother, Sophie Klisman/Zosia/Zysla Tajch speak in November, 2018.

Sophie Tajch Klisman was given an honor to light one of the candles at the Holocaust Memorial Center in Farmington Hills, MI in 2017 at the Yom HaShoah.

4,456 Miles

The upper photo is Lori and Jeff Ellis, Mark Klisman, Sophie Klisman, Michelle Ellis, Joshua and Kelsey Ellis. The lower photo has Sophie Tajch Klisman's two children on the bema.

We were at the Holocaust and Heroism Remembrance Day—Yom HaShoah, 2017.

First row further back: Mark Klisman, Jeff Ellis, Kelsey and Josh Ellis, Marla Shloss. The next row: Anne Klisman, Toby Kuppe (my mother's friend), Sophie Tajch Klisman, Michelle Ellis and Lori Ellis

Chapter 20 Where Do We Go From Here?

*"I am not a victim.
I am a survivor"*

—*anonymous*

We cannot be passive observers. By doing nothing you are in fact taking a stand. You are allowing others to get picked on, bullied, or beaten.

*"We can't live in the past
nor can you change the past.
So never forget
but live in the future."*

—*Dr. Edith Eva Eger*

Accept differences in people and learn from them. One must understand that bullying usually occurs because the person bullying has low self-esteem and he/she thinks it makes them feel more empowered by attacking others. The bullier may be bullied themselves by others.

Where does such hatred come from? Is it instilled in others at such a young age? In certain cultures cartoons are shown to them and the animated characters are using rifles and other weapons to kill the Jews. We must teach our youth to intervene, be tolerant of differences, and enjoy the diversity that life has to offer. My mother always told me life would be so boring if we were all the same. We all must get educated on this topic and help to stop the atrocities that are still occurring in different parts of the world today.

Here are some recommended books to read to help you teach others to stand up for their rights:

- *Stand up for your Rights: Children from all over the World,* illustrated and edited by young people all over the world. This is by World Book Encyclopedia.

- *Stand up for your Life: A Practical Step-By-Step Plan to Build Inner Confidence and Personal Power* by Cheryl Richardson

- *Stand up For Children's Rights.* This is a Teacher's Guide for Exploration and Action with 11-16 year olds, created by Unicef.

There are many wonderful books written for middle schoolers on the Holocaust such as *The Diary of a Young Girl* by Anne Frank
- *The Book Thief* by Markus Zusak
- *Number the Stars* by Lois Lowry
- *The Boy in the Stripped Pajamas* by John Boyne
- *The Boy on the Wooden Box: How the Impossible Became Possible... on Shindler's List* by Leon Leyson

There are many DVD's that go along with these books as well. Of course there are many, many more wonderful books on this topic. Just start googling away.

Soon the 2G and 3G (second and third generation survivors) will have to take over the role of speaking at the Holocaust Memorial Centers.

This is not the end, it is just the beginning of life long lessons to be carried out from one generation to the next. Let us never forget. As Simon Dubnow stated to his fellow prisoners in the ghetto "Jew, write it all down."

New Lodz Cemetery in the Ghetto Fields **(wikimedia)**

*"Let us remember the suffering in order to
appreciate what we have now:
food, shelter, family, love and freedom."*
—**Lori Renay Klisman Ellis**

*"It is deeply shocking and
incomprehensible to me
that despite volumes of documentation
and living witnesses
who can attest to the horrors of the
holocaust, there are
still those who would deny it."*
—**Mark Udall**

*"To forget the dead would be akin to
killing them a second time."*
—**Elie Wiesel**

Chapter 21 How Can An Ordinary Citizen Make An Impact In Eradicating Anti-Semitism?

Dr. Nick Hersh, a local Orthodontist in Michigan as well as a board member and president at the West Bloomfield School District decided to make a difference in our world. He spoke with a friend about his dream of one day teaching English in the Swiss Alps. His friend said what about teaching English in Poland instead. This piqued Nick's interest. He was asked if he would prefer teaching in a big city or little city. He chose a little city named Dobczyce, Poland. Nick knew a big city was familiar with the Jewish population; while a smaller city may not have any exposure to Jews. So in 2012 Nick decided to fly to Dobczyce.

Dobczyce is a town in southern Poland. Cloth and wool making were popular many years ago. Now a days it is a farming community and they grow chocolate. Prior to World War 2 there were 762 Jews in the town. Tragically they all perished when they were forced to go to Auschwitz-Birkenau Concentration and Extermination Camp. When asked if there are any remnants of a Jewish existence, he shared the synagogue was demolished and presently it is a police station. There are burnt cinderblocks of what was once a Mikvah (a bath for Jewish rituals). Nick stated the grounds were filthy so he provided a monetary incentive for the students to clean it up. His aspiration is to restore and memorialize the Mikvah. That would help to educate all the residents in the town about how there once was a Jewish existence there. One of the residents from Dobczyce found a kiddush cup and gave it to Nick. He in turn donated it to the Holocaust Memorial Center, in Farmington Hills, Mi.

Nick is starting to become a familiar face in town. He is well respected and liked by the principal/director of the school and the town's people. He is invited to dinners. He shared he was there during the paczki season and everyone insisted that he eat paczkis.

Nick comes prepared to Dobczyce with his "one way suitcase" filled with "magic pencils" which change colors, pens and t-shirts. His mission was to build a rapport with the 500–600 students he would be teaching, teach the students English, as well as dispel stereotypes about Americans. He wanted to teach them about the diversity in America. This catapulted him into the next conversation. "What do you know about Jewish people?" They shared the stereotypic responses such as being greedy, stingy and counting their money. Nick asked "Do you know any Jewish people?" The students said no. "Why are you lying to me?" That is when he shared that he was Jewish.

Not only was he educating the students, but at times the parents would attend these classes as well. Nick stated there were 150 students in a class, and the next hour the classes were combined into two classes together which allowed Nick to educate 300 students. This continued with another hour of 150 more students. Nick said these 10-16 year olds change their perceptions on Americans and Jews into a positive manner after sitting through his classes. The hope is these students can help to educate their peers. Eventually when the students get married and have children they will educate the next generation. Just imagine 600 students multiplied by 7 years, which comes out to 4,200 students. Then add in thousands of parents as well! Nick feels he is making an immeasurable change in their lives. "I can change the next generation." He feels strongly about the fact if he can make an impact, so can you. Nick is demonstrating altruism and is doing a mitzvah. Hopefully this will motivate others to do a mitzvah as well. Thank you for being the person to make a change in the world!

Nick also helps arrange for the students to take a tour to Auschwitz-Birkenau Concentration and Extermination Camp. Once there, the students partake in the self-guided tours. This tour is so powerful and life changing.

As we know there is still anti-Semitism in Poland. Nick stated there are approximately 5,000 Jews living in Poland today, and many are still discovering that they are of Jewish decent. This was hidden from them, in order to keep them safe. We hope with education, there will be less violent acts against the Jewish population.

Unfortunately in 2018 the Polish Senate passed a bill that made it illegal to accuse the Polish nation or state of being complicit in the Holocaust. The President of Poland feels he has to defend the historical truth. There is a fine or jail time associated with this. Israel as well as many Jews around the world feel this is an attempt to deny the Holocaust and rewrite history. Just ask any survivor if the poles helped the Jews. Luckily, this law was revoked.

Part VIII: Finding New Family

Chapter 22 Online Groups

In March, 2017 I joined several Jewish online sites from Facebook such as *Children of Holocaust Survivors, Generations of the Shoah International (GSI), Tracing the Tribe- Jewish Genealogy of Facebook* and more. One day I responded to a message on the Lodz JRI-Poland website regarding a husband who wanted to find a tour guide for his wife who would be going to Lodz all alone. I wrote that I was there putting up a tombstone for the Tajch family at the New Lodz Cemetery and would check to see if our driver Kasha was available. Unfortunately she was not. A few days later, to my surprise I received an email from the wife of the man I was corresponding with. As Rebecca Rosen says there are no coincidences in life. This must be a spiritual connection to make me respond to his post. The email was from a woman name, Michelle Minya Tajch Scorecroft and she wrote "We may be family."

So who is Michelle Minya Tajch? She lived in Cambridge while her husband was an assistant professor. What a coincidence that Josh studied abroad in Cambridge. Now she lives in both Paris and London. She was a social worker and retired. She is now a writer. Her father was Hindrick Tajch born in Lodz, Poland. Nowhere on the family tree does it show up that we have someone with that name. She went back to Poland to find her ancestry just like I did. She does not have a lot of information on him because he died at a young age, and her mother got remarried.

She was going to go to the Lodz Cemetery and try to locate family with the last name "Tajch" as well as put up a stone for my grandmother Liba Tajch; however she could not find a guide to take her to the exact spot. She was disappointed that no one was there to help her, as well as the fact that she has some difficulty ambulating and the terrain was rather uneven and rough for her. She corresponded with me, in the beginning almost daily, about how emotional a journey this was. She did not go with her husband because he is not Jewish and she did not feel she needed him there. She was surprised that her father was from Lodz, because she initially thought he was from another town in Poland. When she got to the other town and looked at the records she realized there was no one there with the name Tajch.

Can we be related somehow? I think we may possibly be cousins. She feels we look alike. She stated in her younger days

4,456 Miles

there was a strong resemblance. I do feel a closeness to her. Who knows—one day when I go back to London and Paris I may contact her.

Chapter 23 The Family Is Growing
70 years later I found more Tajch family (family in Uruguay and Israel)

On August 7, 2018 my mother Sophie Klisman and sister-in-law Anne Klisman came over for lunch. I was excited to share my genealogy research with them. I recently joined the World Ancestry online and thought I found a link with my grandmother Liba Rozrazowsk. I clicked on her name because it had a green leaf and lo and behold there was another man named Alan Theirman who also had Rozrazowska in his family. I contacted him immediately.

I noticed he lived in Boyton Beach, Florida. Since Mom vacations in Boca Raton, I was hoping they could meet and talk about family. I was hoping there would be a strong connection. I searched his family tree for photos of Liba but had no luck. I was so hopeful this connection would lead to a relationship and answers. Alan emailed me back after 5 hours and said he was related to the Weiskopf family and one of the Weiskopfs married a Rozrazoska. He said he was still trying to get more information on the Weiskopf side. That was it. I was disappointed.

After lunch I told my mother and Anne to come to the office and look at the family tree. I said we now have many generations of relatives. My mother said it does not mean a lot to her to have 4th and 5th generation relatives, but she would be so happy to have contact with her Tajch relatives from Uruguay. I told her several years ago I made an effort to search "Skype" for all family with the last name of Tajch. Since it is a rare name I had an inkling that whomever I attempted to contact was family. I gave it my best shot. So in Spanish I sent out several messages on Skype.

For example I wrote "Hola, mi llama es Lori. Yo vivo en USA. Me Madre's llamo es Tajch. Su familia es mi familia," etc. There was no response. A few weeks later, I attempted to contact them but shortly after I received a message from Skype that I am sending out too many messages or I am disturbing people. I surprisingly did get one response from an Augustin Tajch. He and I started to correspond and I found out that he lived in Montevideo, Uruguay.

He shared with me he only met his father twice. His mother had a relationship with Dr. Mauricio Tajch. However, Dr. Mauricio Tajch was married. He and I corresponded occasionally on Facebook. Over the years Augustin moved to California with his wife and became a magician. He posts frequently and he is into body building.

So this brings me back to August 7, 2018 when I sent out a new Skype message to Gabriela Tajch. Although it stated she lived in "IL", I figured her name sounded like it could be of a South American origin. Anne googled the country code IL and found out it was Israel.

Anne contacted her cousin Anita. She asked Anita to find Gabriela's number and call her. Anita made an attempt to get her number but did not have any success through that avenue. She however had success with a Facebook search. She left her a private message. Next Anita googled her name and found an obituary article on her father "Dr. Mauricio Tajch." Although that article was in Spanish it allowed for an English translation. We hit the jackpot on this one.

It stated Dr. Mauricio Tajch died 10 years ago and listed his wife Rebeca, his daughter Gabriella and husband, and his son Marcel. With this new information I proceeded to private message Gabriela and then made an attempt with Marcel. In the message I stated their grandfather Israel Tajch was born in Poland and left to go to Uruguay, South America before WWII. I said their grandfather had several siblings but one was Berek Icek Tajch. Berek was my mother's father. I said that after the war Israel Tajch came to the USA to meet up with his nieces Sophie and Felicia.

On another occasion their father Dr. Mauricio Tajch and his mother Rebeca came to New York and met with my Aunt Felicia and Uncle Roman. Israel gave one picture to my mother. It was a photo of him and his daughter at his daughter's wedding. This information was enough to pique an interest in both Marcel and Gabriela.

Marcel wrote back to me on Facebook's private messenger within 5 minutes. Not only did he write to me but he sent me voice messages. I also asked for pictures of his family. I received a picture of his father, grandfather, himself, his mother and wedding photos. This was an amazing success! Marcel said he was elated and excited to talk to me. He said he was in the stars!

Next, Gabriela wrote back to me. She was also excited that I found her and connected with her. She has three sons and one is an archeologist and one is a musician. The musician Andres has some health issues she is dealing with. I told her I would be in Israel in May and love to meet her. She said she is living day by day due to

4,456 Miles

the health issues and it does not sound like she can commit at this point. I gave her my cell number and asked if she was on WhatsApp. She told me to email her mother and send her our conversations.

On August 9, 2018 my cell phone rang in the morning and it was a call from Uruguay. She spoke in English and asked if I knew who this was. I said yes I know. Is it Rebeca? She said yes. She was excited to speak to me. She is 82 years old, an attorney and will email me. She sounded excited to keep in touch. I invited the family to come to the USA and stay with us. I hope to keep this relationship going since we have such a small family. Stay tuned for hopefully more information. Rebeca sent me her email address. She is also on Whats App?

So the plan to visit with Gabriela Tajch in Jerusalem in May fell through. Unfortunately Gabriela was unable to meet with me but I plan to keep connected with our family.

Above: Rebeca Tajch and her daughter Gabriela Tajch

Right: Gabriela's boys Adrian, Nicholas, Andre (in Israel)

Lori Klisman Ellis

Right: Rebeca's son Marcel Tajch (Uruguay)

Top left: Marcel and his father Mauricio

Bottom left: Mauricio and Rebeca Tajch's family in Uruguay. Marcel's grandfather Israel Tajch is at the far left

Rebeca & Mauricio Tajch

Chapter 24 The Family Continues To Grow

Let me start by saying my family grew on June 30, 2018. We added a beautiful daughter-in-law to our family. Joshua Ellis married Kelsey Prena. We were thrilled to have her in our family.

Photo taken at University Club, In East Lansing Michigan, June 30, 2018

I was also excited to receive an email from David Weiskopf from Southern Maryland, about an hour away from D.C. He noticed we were connected on his family tree through the Weiskopf side. This was the initial email:

"Just thought I would say hi. I see that you descend from Berek Wajskopf. I descend from his brother Mosiek Wajskopf. Together with a descendant of Berek Wajskopf, Nir Waiskopf- we have researched and put up a large tree of Wajskopfs from the Czestochowa area. Again, just wanted to say hi and that it is nice to see that another line of the family is still around! Berek's father was Michal Wajskopf and he was born around 1730, not sure where but we know that he died in a little village outside of Czestochowa called Kokawa in 1826 when he was 96 years old." Best, David Weiskopf

Lori Klisman Ellis

Well this certainly piqued my interest. I emailed him back immediately. I found out that in November, 2017 he was 48 years old, married and has a four year old. A newborn arrived in 2018. He is a lawyer for the local government and teaches business law and business ethics for UMUC. David stated he may be my 5th cousin since our lines diverged in the early 1800's. His 5th great grandfather Mosiek Wajskopf was brothers with Berek Wajskopf that I descended from.

He mentioned Nir Waiskopf from Jerusalem, Israel also descended from the Berek line. We have been in touch. I asked him about family reunions and he stated years ago he used to participate in them. He has family in New Mexico and all over the world so it is hard to plan these things now, since he works a lot and has children.

I just got another message from an Ancestry user stating our DNA matched. This was a man named Sid Liebowitz. He is retired now but used to work for Donald Trump at the Trump Tower. Sid stated he was the VP for Trump Tower. He negotiated deals. He shared some very confidential information with me about Donald Trump. For legal purposes, I will not disclose that information in this book at the present time until it is verified. Sid stated he is a "Level" genealogist, so he is available for his cousins if we need assistance with research. He told me we matched on the Wajskop side of the family.

Every few months I receive additional correspondences from future relatives. I find it fascinating that my family is growing.

Well Nir met with Anne, Sophie and me in Jerusalem. He is a very intelligent man. He received a PhD in Chemistry. He is a warm and kind relative. Nir was very easy to talk to. He brought his laptop to share his family tree with us. He also shared a family montage he created for his father's 70th birthday.

Sophie, Nir, and Lori

Part IX: Preparing For The 2019 FIDF Mission To Poland/Israel

Chapter 25 Mom Is Going On An Incredible Mission!

*"Believe in the power of the individual
to make a difference in this world"*

—Vera Federman

Prior to turning this manuscript into the publisher in January, I thought to myself should I delay turning in the book and wait a few months to hear whether my mother was selected to be the speaker for the FIDF (Friends of Israel Defense Forces) 2019 Mission. I was told after Mom's interview with the Marketing Director of FIDF that she "blew her away." She said she would be informed by the end of December or beginning of January. Mid to late January rolls around and still no word. So I turned in the manuscript and took out the chapter labeled 2019 Mission to Poland and Israel.

On January 28, 2019, The Holocaust Independence Day as well as the liberation of Auschwitz comes and my husband and I and my brother and sister-in-law go to the Holocaust Memorial Center in Farmington Hills to watch a viewing of a movie about the hidden chronicles of Poland that transpired during the underground movement in the Warsaw ghetto with Emanuel Ringelblum. It was a poignant, heart wrenching story with live video footage. I along with my family came home depressed. We had a new and more vivid understanding of the tragedies my parents went through during the ghetto.

Shortly after I received a phone call from my friend Paula Lebowitz, the Director of the Michigan Chapter of the FIDF. She shared that she was in a meeting in Florida with the Director of Marketing and with Major General Meir Klifi-Amir. They approached him and asked if a survivor was chosen for the mission. He said not yet, and then the two woman shared what a wonderful survivor Mom was and retold her life story. That is when Major General Klifi agreed to having both my mother and another survivor from Israel go on the mission and be the speakers for the 2019 Mission to Poland and Israel.

I was elated! I shared the wonderful news with her chaperone, Anne Klisman. It is such a comfort knowing that Mom will be surrounded by love and support of 50 Israeli soldiers and from Anne during this arduous mission.

I was told not to call Mom, but that Paula Lebowitz wanted to call and share the wonderful news with her. I knew Mom would be excited. She called me right after and was indeed elated. She will now be known as an International Holocaust Speaker. The FIDF will plan to take photos of her when she returns from Florida to advertise the mission. She will be educating the world.

I had plans to go to Israel for the first time with my husband and with four other couples on our own mission. The dates would overlap her trip. I was so disappointed that I could not join her trip, but thrilled my sister-in-law would accompany her. I also invited my children to join the FIDF mission, if they could take time off of work.

I am so excited to hear about the next chapter of Zysla Tajch/Sophie Klisman's journey in life. I truly believe this will aid in her healing process even more than the 2016 trip to Poland did for her. She has spoken more in Michigan to groups of students in the Holocaust Memorial Center. She has gone back to Auschwitz and survived it. She is getting stronger and more powerful as she ages. She is invincible! She is my hero. Who else at the age of 89½ has the physical strength and emotional courage to travel around the world not as a tourist but as an educator, leader and a survivor?

Yesterday I called my brother and sister-in-law and told them I was corresponding with the staff via email at Salzwedel. I began my correspondences several weeks ago. I was interested to learn if there were photos of my mother and Aunt Felicia there or any documents. I also informed them that my mother was still alive and of course a survivor of their work camp. They sent me some documents they had on both of them, which was limited. It was accurate information on them but nothing new. They asked if my mother would be willing to fly to Salzwedel and speak at the 74th International Holocaust Remembrance Day. What an honor to be asked. They would pay for her and a companion to fly there. She was honored but had a prior commitment to speak in Poland/Israel.

My mother shared that she remembered a lot about Salzwedel with the woman guards. She said one guard had a heart when she collapsed and let her go back to sleep. But within a few minutes another woman guard without a heart dragged her out of her sleep, beat her and swore at her the whole way to the munitions factory. She also mentioned that she recalls vividly the liberation of Salzwedel. She said she was at that camp the longest, possibly 9

4,456 Miles

months. I suggested that hopefully next year she would be able to go and speak!

After reviewing the email from Salzwedel I clicked on one of the links that was sent to me, which redirected me to the ITS (International Tracing service). There I checked if any family member had possessions that their heirs can claim. There were photos of watches and other smaller items. The items that were not claimed were displayed at Holocaust Museums. I had no luck finding any items for Tajch, Rozrazowska, Klisman, Shloss, etc.

I continued to search on the ITS site again and checked for missing people. I once again put in Israel Tajch/Izrael Teich and just Tajch but did not find anything. I searched in Rozrazowska but no information was found. When I searched for Klisman, to my surprise Leon popped up. I clicked "search for additional family members" with the name Klisman and found information on Benek Klisman and Jakob Klisman. There was even a photo of my Uncle Leon. It is the same photo that hangs on my wall in my office at home. Leon stated he wanted to come to Canada on the papers. Unfortunately my dad Benek, Leon, and Jakob did not go to Canada, but rather Leon and Jakob went to Australia and my dad came to the USA. I shared all the information I found online with my brother Mark, sister-in-law Anne, and my mother Sophie.

Spiritual Moment:
The next morning I got a phone call from Anne. She stated in the middle of the night she heard a bang on the wall in her house. It was a horribly windy and cold night, with wind chills as low as -35 degrees. What she found was the photo of Uncle Leon popped off the wall and was on her floor. She laughed and told me I would get a kick out of it. She said Uncle Leon was mad that Anne did not research him online, but only Lori did. I think he knows we are thinking about him, and that Anne and Mom are planning a journey back to Poland/Israel.

Stay tuned for exciting things to come in preparation of Sophie and Anne's FIDF mission to Poland and Israel.

Now that I know Mom and Anne will be going to Poland and Israel I started making contact with our new family members: Gabriela Tajch, her mother Rebeca Tajch, and Nir Weiskopf. Unfortunately Rebeca Tajch is not able to meet us in Israel as she lives in South America and only goes to Israel once a year in October for Gabriela's birthday. Gabriela cannot meet us. I also sent an email to Nir asking if he could meet us in Jerusalem as well. He said he would love to meet us.

Each day that passes Mom said she is training for a marathon. Although it is not really a marathon, she is taking more exercise classes at the clubhouse and walking more to be fit for Poland and Israel. She takes a yoga class, tai chi and more. She shared with me that tai chi is so slow moving. She asked the instructor if it will pick up and get faster. The instructor told her it was for people who had arthritis and needed practice with balance. I guess my near 90 year old mother should be in classes with 20 year olds! She is determined to be in great shape for this trip.

As the date is quickly approaching she has been busy with radio interviews, interviews from the news, and meeting with a solider from the 84th infantry. It has been a whirlwind of publicity. She is also busy packing and emotionally preparing what to say on her trip. I know she will be fabulous. She has the physical and emotional attributes to succeed on this journey. Her family and friends are all so proud of her. Let the journey begin!

4,456 Miles

Part X: Public Relations Information On Sophie Klisman

Chapter 26 Newspapers, The News, Videos & Radio Stations

The Public Relations person from the Friends of the Israel Defense Forces is doing a great job. My mother is receiving requests to be interviewed by several different sources. You can view her at the following sites:
• *The Jewish News*—April 4-10, 2019 edition and May 20-24, 2019 edition.
• Detroitnews.com April 17, 2019. She can be viewed online.
• Her story was in the *Detroit News* on April 18, 2019. https://www.detroitnews.com/story/news/local/oakland-county/2019/04/17/holocaust-survivors-trip-link-jewish-past-present/3430555002
• NBC Detroit with Steve Garagiola.
• A radio interview was held with Denny Gillem from *Frontlines of Freedom* radio show. Her condensed story and other people that were interviewed was aired on April 28-29, 2019 at 11:00 p.m.–1:00 p.m. A podcast was made available on April 30, 2019.

She will now be able to share her story with thousands of viewers. My hope is twofold:
1. It continues to help in her healing process and
2. Her story helps to eradicate anti-Semitism.

I also received a request to write a blog about my mother's story from Swenja Granzow-Rauwald. She works for the Neuengamme Memorial on educational projects, holds seminars and other activities for descendants. She runs a multi-lingual Reflections blog. (http://reflections.news). It was the May 4, 2019 issue called *Protected: From Silence to Commemorating Together as a Family*. A hard copy of the blog can also be viewed in the second book *Ellis/Klisman Family Tree*, under Zysla Tajch/Sophie Klisman.

In addition an article about my mother was written for the *Hedim/Voice's* November 2019 issue for the town of Piotrkow. That article can be viewed online as well. The website is www.piotrkow-jc.com

My mother's video and life story was also shared with the Salzwedel Museum. They will air it at their 74th liberation ceremony.

175

Sophie is on YouTube: https://www.youtube.com/watch?v= uyjK5VSA-R8 or, if you google YouTube and add Sophie Klisman's name you will find her story.

Sophie was interviewed by Mitch Albom on 4-18-2019 on WJR Radio. To hear her interview you can google WJR and go to Mitch Albom's podcast.

After the *Detroit News* article was published, Gregg Krupa the author of the article received an email from Douglas J. Harvey. Mr. Harvey was a soldier who was in the 84th Infantry in Germany, at Salzwedel during the time of my mother's liberation (April 14, 1945). He emailed the following information:

Douglas J.Harvey, PFC Head Quarters Company First Battalion 334th Regiment 84th Infantry Division

"I read the article on Sophie Klisman with great interest as I was with the 84th Infantry Division that liberated the Salzwedel Camp. I have several pictures from our Division History one which is attached. I was not one of the GIs on the tanks she described but was in the column a few hundred yards behind. I remember well the happy women on the road waving at us. It was the only time in our fight across Germany when we received such a welcome. I also attached my picture taken within days of the Salzwedel liberation."

Another correspondence on April 18, 2019 from Douglas Harvey was as follows: *"I remember all these women coming out on the street. I was on our truck pulling an antitank gun. The Guys riding the tanks*

4,456 Miles

were from our Battalion Rifle Companies. I did see one of our men holding up a whip that he had just liberated from the camp. I think we only stopped briefly and moved on to the bank of the Elbe River to await the arrival of the Russians. The Division also liberated Ahlem near Hannover where lack of food was very evident. I would be happy to meet with your family. As you know the WW2 soldiers are rapidly moving on. This month I will be 95 but I think I am in reasonable good physical and mental health."

—Doug Harvey

We are hoping to meet with this hero in person! We just received confirmation that the Detroit Newspaper wants to do a story on Douglas J. Harvey, the man in the 84th infantry and my mother, the survivor.

Here are some additional articles, videos and speaking engagements about my mother and some with my mother and her liberator (links active at the time of publication):

- https://apnews.com/1ed3e81f14b94d1b9796e76ef1487e7b
- https://www.yahoo.com/news/holocaust-survivor-former-soldier-emotional-meeting-202742579.html
- https://www.foxnews.com/us/holocaust-survivor-former-soldier-have-emotional-meeting
- https://www.washingtonpost.com/national/holocaust-survivor-former-soldier-have-emotional-meeting/2019/05/13/f9d17ae6-75bd-11e9-a7bf-c8a43b84ee31_story.html?utm_term=.7a70d2c56434
- https://www.detroitnews.com/story/news/local/oakland-county/2019/05/13/holocaust-survivor-meets-ex-gi-you-gave-me-my-life/1128611001/
- https://thejewishnews.com/2019/05/14/survivor-and-liberator-meet-after-74-years/
- My mother was also featured on NBC news (channel 4) in West Bloomfield, MI. on May 14, 2019.
- On May 17, my mother spoke at the Holocaust Memorial Center to a large group of people. In the group was George Takei, Lieutenant Sulu from the original Star Trek TV show.

177

- She was also featured on Fox national news on May 17, 2019 by Martha MacCallum which can be view at: https://youtu.be/J0RxwqoF2FA
- Sophie is also featured in the Friends of Israel Defense Forces website at http://www.fidf.org/news/hol...
- Sophie's blog was shared on April 11, 2019 at https://www.facebook.com/pg/rfhabnc/posts/

Sophie posing with her son Mark on the left, her daughter Lori in the middle, and her daughter-in-law Anne on the right, each holding a photo of Sophie's four grandkids. From L to R: Rachel Klisman, Michelle Ellis, Joshua Ellis and Aaron Klisman.

My mother thanked Doug Harvey, one of the liberators from the 84th infantry for giving her a life. Because of him she was able to get married, have children and grandchildren.

Part XI: 84th Infantry Soldier Meets Survivor

Chapter 27 The Long Anticipated Reunion

On April 28, 2019 Sophie Klisman, Jeff and I met Mom's hero; her liberator from the 84th infantry that gave her an opportunity for a new life.

Doug Harvey, 95 year old who received his PhD from MSU in Engineering is a kind, educated, humble, intelligent man. He does not take much credit for his role in liberating Mom and the 2,999 other prisoners in Salzwedel. He said he was just doing his job.

Doug stated "By the time I arrived in Germany, the soldiers were surrendering to me." There were tens of thousands of German soldiers surrendering. The 84th infantry captured the largest amount of prisoners.

"When Hitler died the war was over. This was the total collapse of the German soldiers." Doug stated that on May 7, 1945 the war was officially over. There was minimal resistance and the Germans were waving the white flags. It was quiet in the day but at night there was still a little resistance. They knew the American soldiers would not kill them, but the Germans were worried that the Russian soldiers would kill them. Doug said he saved some German soldiers from getting shot. He claims he could not hurt anyone, not even an insect. He cannot comprehend how some people could do such harm to innocent lives.

Doug Harvey graduated from high school at the age of 17 and for a year and a half he worked for Ford Dealership before he started college at MSU. At MSU he was in ROTC. He decided to enlist in the reserves because his father and uncles also served. If he did not enlist he would have been drafted.

With only two semesters complete at MSU he received the call that he was needed right away. He was in the AST (Army Specialized Training Program) at Drexel for a short time. The staff realized he had a good aptitude in mechanics and they wanted to train him in this area. Then he also took an exam in the medical area and the staff realized he had a good aptitude in that area as well. Doug said it would have been difficult working in medicine as he would have to take care of the wounded soldiers, so he opted to pursue mechanics. Shortly after he was called on to be part of the 84th infantry.

Doug remembers railroads being bombed near Salzwedel. He remembers the bombing near the airport there as well. My mother said she heard the bombing and knew the Germans would not be bombing themselves. She along with Aunt Felicia had a feeling the allies were near. They kept holding on another day and another day until their freedom came.

Another vivid memory Doug had was that one of his peers from the 84th infantry opened the gates of Salzwedel and let all the woman out of the camp. Then the soldier found the whips used by Nazi guards. That soldier took one and circled it in the air after the gates were open. My mother said she was fortunate never to have been whipped.

When asked how long Doug was at Salzwedel, he said not long at all. The platoon continued going south to liberate a nearby men's camp. He said the men were wearing striped uniforms and were emaciated and near death.

Doug was curious how conditions were after the 84th infantry left. My mother shared that the woman were provided food but they had to learn how to eat again. According to records that Doug had, public order needed be established. A "burgermeister" was appointed who hired a police force. The policemen had to find a way to obtain clothing and food for the displaced persons and allied POWs. They also had to remove the German soldiers from hospitals and allow allied soldiers to come in and do jobs. There were assignments to get bunk beds, clean up the cemetery, and more.

Doug said there were 30 men in his platoon in the 84th infantry. One was killed. Three were missing in action, but after the war two of the men were found and alive. Doug initially contemplated shooting himself in the foot to get out of the war because he was worried he would not make it out alive. He was fired at, slept in the trenches, and lived in freezing cold conditions outside. At times he had hot meals while other times he ate from cans.

When Sophie asked if he killed any Nazi soldiers, he said he hit a tank with his anti-tank gun, but he never brutalized any prisoners. "I don't think I killed anyone. They just surrendered to me."

Doug shared photos of Salzwedel with us, photos of himself as Private Doug in his uniform. He shared books and gave us several books to review and then donate to the Holocaust Memorial Center. He had a book on Kissinger as well. He gave us the 84th infantry seal called the "railsplitters."

4,456 Miles

After two hours my mother again reiterated this statement, which was extremely powerful: "You gave me a chance for a new, normal life. Thank you. You are my hero!"

Doug Harvey, Liberator and Sophie Tajch Klisman, Survivor April 28, 2019

Doug, at 95 years old, is an independent, alert, intelligent and gentle soul. He is extremely humble and did not want to take credit for his work because there were 15,000 men in the 84th unit. He said he was just doing his job. He said "I cannot hurt a spider, so for me to be in the war and have to fire a rifle was tough."

"I do not know if I killed anyone, but I did hit a tank. You could not pay me a million dollars to do this job but it was worth a million dollars to save all those lives which were imprisoned." After our meeting with Doug, he posted a photo of my mother and himself on a Facebook page called the 84th Infantry *Railsplitter*.

James Spohn in the 84th infantry

He received several comments, but one stood out. It was a comment from David Spohn. He wrote the following: "My dad was Pfc. James F. Spohn, Headquarters Company, 1st Battalion - 333rd Infantry. For much of the war he was in Signal Corps. Mr. Spohn wrote this information on Salzwedel:

"In a small German town called Salzwedel we came upon a women's concentration camp. We learned later that this group of prisoners included about 2,700 Jewish women from Eastern Europe and 300 non-Jewish women political prisoners from Western Europe. They burst out of their camp when the gates were opened and straggled en masse down the main street of the town clad in dark blue or striped uniforms, each uniform with a large yellow "X" on its back a few inches below the shoulder blades. The yellow X on the uniforms provided the German guards with a target, should a prisoner try to escape.

"The women broke windows in the bakeries and shops and grabbed loaves of bread and other food. They didn't seem to have any individuality—just a horde of desperate people. They looked gaunt, if not starved. We knew they were women, but they had little appearances of femininity. Our American soldiers literally backed away from them—almost horrified by what they saw. The last I saw of these wretched women, they were slowly filtering off into the shops and alleys as they ran out of steam. It was an awesome sight and caused our crew to wonder again what kind of people the Germans really were.

"It wasn't until almost 25 years later that I realized the full enormity of the German oppression of these women. By chance, I happened then to watch a documentary produced by BBC television. The documentary related the history of a group of women—describing the majority of them as Polish Jews—who had been held for a long

time in concentration camps in Eastern Germany. As the Russians advanced in the spring of 1945, the women were forced to march hundreds of miles to the west at a large loss of life. The memoir was on the Salzwedel prisoners."

I emailed David and we also spoke on the phone. He told me this is such as emotional experience knowing that his father probably met my mother and helped liberate her. I asked if he could fly to Walled Lake, MI on May 13, 2019 and meet my mother, Doug Harvey and the Detroit News. He should bring a photo of his father, another war hero! He said he would be there and he was at this emotional reunion.

Mr. Henry Kissinger is on the left and Mr. James Spohn is on the right.

James Spohn was a switch board operator in the war. He was roommates with Henry Kissinger. James became an attorney, just like his father. James got married and had David and two daughters.

They grew up next door to a Catholic man who was born in Poland and was imprisoned in Auschwitz. David said his neighbor talked about the Holocaust a lot while James rarely did. Although while in school James had a writing assignment and wrote a 40 page article about his experience in the war. He made a powerful statement "That the war was worth fighting!"

David's father would be proud of David sharing his story. I am so thankful for men like James. He put his own life on the line to save others. Without his assistance my mother may never have been liberated. David Spohn along with Sophie Klisman are featured in an article in the May issue of the *Detroit News* and *Jewish News*.

Henry Kissinger was also part of the 84th infantry. It became apparent quite quickly how intelligent Kissinger was and he was assigned to organize the government and be a translator in the army. After serving, Fritz Kraemer suggested Kissinger study politics and history and we all know where he ended up—Harvard. Kissinger was in the 335th division which liberated Ahlem concentration camp on April 10, 1945. Four days later the 33rd division liberated Salzwedel.

Kissinger described what the survivors of Ahlem looked like: "Cloth seemed to fall from the bodies, the head was held up by a stick that once might have been a throat. Poles hang from the sides where arms should be, poles are the legs." They had "empty faces and dead eyes." One soldier from Kissinger's infantry arrived inside a hut where forced laborers worked and said "we had to kick them to tell the dead from the living."

Kissinger commented on one particular survivor. He stated "Your foot has been crushed so that you can't run away, your face is 40, your body is ageless, yet all your birth certificate reads is 16." (Online article from Tabletmag.com called "Kissinger on liberating Ahlem Concentration Camp" by Menachem Butler October 29, 2015). This is probably a universal description on how horrific the other survivors looked in all the other concentration camps.

Part XII:
Poland & Israel FIDF Mission
May 2–May 10, 2019

Chapter 28 Sophie Klisman's Trifold Mission: Educate, Eradicate Hate & Get Closure

And so the journey begins. On April 30, 2019 Sophie Tajch Klisman and Anne Klisman are off to Poland and then to Israel. Coincidentally, Jeff and Lori Ellis along with four other couples are off to Israel on the same day. Once again, there are feelings of excitement and trepidation. I just learned there was another anti-Semitic incident in San Diego, California. An armed gunmen came in to the Chabad Poway Synagogue and killed one Jewish woman and injured three people. One was an eight year old girl and her nephew. The man and his niece moved here from Israel. They lived close to the Gaza strip and they were afraid of all the missiles being shot into Israel. So they moved to California to be safer. How tragic that this happened yet again on US soil or that it is still happening. Is there anywhere in the world that is safe? I'm hoping for a safe and unbelievable journey to Israel. The next time I get to this book will be when we all return from our missions. When we return, my mother has to meet with the Detroit news with Doug Harvey for a story, and two appearances on the news. I wish her all the best!

We returned from an incredible journey. While my mother and Anne were in Poland telling her powerful story in Auschwitz, Jeff and I, along with four other couples were in Israel while rockets were being fired into the southern area. We had a tour in Ashdod two days prior to this spot where 90 rockets were fired. Thank goodness we were heading to the northern area as things escalated. The next day there were 150 additional rockets being fired and then the following day there were approximately 900 rockets. I was fearful as one rocket made it 12 miles west of Jerusalem. Fortunately they agreed to a cease fire prior to my mother and Anne arriving in Israel.

Although emotional and difficult to share her story, I was informed that my mother was articulate and had excellent recall of information. The FIDF was there to provide financial support for Israel, educate the delegation on the need to continue to support the soldiers and Israel, provide compassion and love to the survivors and much more. My mother received rave reviews when I met the

FIDF staff. Paula even thought she could be a spokesperson for the FIDF. I think my mother just wants to go back to her quiet and calm life. She went above and beyond her dream of becoming a teacher and educating the world.

Some of the highlights of my mother's mission include arriving in the beautiful country of Israel. She stated if Israel would have been a country prior to 1939 the Holocaust may never have occurred.

Another highlight was meeting the beautiful, young, strong and brave soldiers of the IDF. Anne shared with me this statement "The soldiers said that knowing what she went through, makes them even stronger as soldiers, as they know what they are striving/fighting for."

My mother shared at Shabbat services she was dancing with the soldiers and said "I am having the time of my life." She went from darkness in Poland to light in Israel. Anne stated "Mom went from the deepest of sadness, to the joy of celebrating Shabbat. This is what survivors do: they remember, they move forward, and they find Joy."

Above left: Meeting the young and handsome soldiers. (Sophie said he looks like Paul Newman). Above right: Meeting and getting to know Major General Klifi and the rest of the delegation.

In the evening another one of Sophie's highlights was celebrating life with all the FIDF people. She enjoyed dinner, drinking wine, dancing with the soldiers (doing the hora and being lifted on the chair as if she was having a Bat Mitzvah.)

My mother along with the FIDF surprised me with a blessing from the Rabbi and his wife at the King David Hotel in Jerusalem. She is so thoughtful. She knew I contemplated having a Bat Mitzvah so she wanted to do something special for me.

She said a very difficult experience was arriving in Zbylitowska Gora Village and Buczyna Forest. This is where the murder of 8,000 people occurred and 800 of them were children. Each of the FIDF participants were handed a photo of a child that perished in the forest. It was an emotional day for all.

It was also very difficult for her to return to Poland and speak at Auschwitz-Birkenau Concentration and Extermination Camp. As Major General Klifi stated "It was a cold and miserable day. I was cold and wet but knew I should not complain because I could leave there and be warm and dry for the rest of the day, and I was hungry but I knew I could leave and have food." He said my mother was his hero. Everyone was in awe of her.

Finally Mom achieved the gift of a lifetime: she finally felt safe and at peace. She is considered a hero by all! Mission accomplished!!

Lori emailed a letter to Major General Klifi

"Dear Major General Klifi,

It was a pleasure meeting you and the FIDF staff in Israel. You were very warm and welcoming to my husband Jeff, myself and of course to my mother Sophie Klisman and my sister-in-law, Anne Klisman. It was a life changing experience for my mother.

I wanted to acknowledge Paula Lebowitz for seeking my mother out and giving her this opportunity to share her story with the FIDF and the world. Paula had the faith in my mother's ability to share her experiences during the Holocaust. I am so grateful to Paula and the rest of the FIDF staff for sending Sophie and Anne on this unbelievable mission. By retelling her story she hopefully will have some closure in regards to the Holocaust and be instrumental in educating others about the atrocities of prejudice and anti-Semitism.

Paula went above and beyond her job responsibilities of fundraising to help out in marketing. She helped to orchestrate a meeting with my mother and her liberator with Channel 4, Associated Press, the Jewish News and the Detroit News, with photographers, videographers and others. Paula is extremely capable and professional. She is also empathetic to survivors, soldiers and everyone. I am sure you realize what a true asset she is to the FIDF team. I am very fortunate to call her my friend. So thank you Major General Klifi, Paula and the rest of the FIDF staff on giving my mother and Anne this unbelievable opportunity. We are grateful for all you do to help support Israel and these wonderful soldiers."

Todah
Lori Klisman Ellis

Major General Klifi responded with the following email:

"It was our great honor and pleasure to share this life-altering journey From Holocaust to Independence Mission, together with your amazing mother.

Your mother's presence and testimony about her life during the darkest days of humanity was the central theme leading our mission. Your mother, as you know, is a remarkable woman, whose passion and strength inspired us all. Sharing her story provided context and proportion to our lives and most important, your mother's impression on each and every soldier was so impactful and meaningful. When I asked the soldiers what is their greatest takeaway from their journey, their answer, each, was that they gained a better understanding of their role, responsibilities and mission as soldiers in the IDF to protect the Jewish people around the globe and to ensure NEVER AGAIN.

In your letter you wrote that you hope your mother had some closure from this mission experience. I want to let you know that during the mission your mother shared with me that marching through the gates of Auschwitz, with IDF officers in uniform, carrying the flag of Israel, was so powerful and meaningful to her. My response was that I'm sure that unlike the past, this time, when we marched together through the gates to Auschwitz - Birkenau camp, she knew that she would be walking out of the gates- safe, proud and with a feeling of triumph. I really hope that she was empowered by the resilience and fortitude that she demonstrated to all of us and was able to bring her memories to a level of peace.

Having journeyed to Auschwitz and Israel together with your mother on this mission, commemorating both Yom HaShoah (Holocaust Remembrance Day) and Yom HaZikaron (Israel's Memorial Day), gave all of us a better understanding of the connection between the two memorial days, Yom HaZikaron which reminds us the cost of having Israel, and Yom HaShoah, which reminds us the cost of not!" Lori, I welcome you and your family with open arms to the FIDF family. With gratitude and friendship.

Klifi

My mother compared Major General Klifi to the fruit, Sabra. "It is a prickly pear cactus which has a tough skin on the outside but sweet on the inside. He must be a tough leader yet he shows warmth and love. He is such a kind and loving man."

Chapter 29 Reflections Of The Mission
by Anne Klisman

I felt so happy as I watched my "mom" have fun. I even said it was like her Bat Mitzvah. She looked more "free" and open in her celebration with the IDF young people, their leaders and our group.

While I knew she had strength and spirit, I had never seen her so able to let go and enjoy. When asked my reflection by the videographer I called her Bubbie. I woke up in the middle of the night thinking that might be weird if someone saw the video and I wished I could restate and say "mom" but I want to explain: I think I did that for a couple of reasons. First, we often use Bubbie almost as a name, to tell stories or refer to her. But I realized it was more. I was talking to her four grandchildren. I wished the grandkids along with Lori and her husband Jeff and my husband Mark could feel and experience the openness and fearlessness mom/Sophie was feeling.

And I had an epiphany in the middle of the night. My true reflection came to me. Sophie/mom felt safe. She has even said "Israel makes me feel safe" (these words were stated in Poland). "These beautiful, young faces..." And then I realized mom felt 100% safe. She does not often display this. It is Israel and it is the IDF that gave her the freedom yesterday to let go of her inhibitions and experience complete safety, respect and love!

The IDF young people were strong, but they are soft. They were warm and loving, but you felt/heard they can be tough to protect and honor their

Lori Klisman Ellis

country. To protect all Jewish people and the right to be respected. But they can dance, celebrate, and laugh and be kids too.

I want to add their maturity to communicate with adults like Mom and me is remarkable. They can flip from being strong, adult behaving soldiers to dancing giggling kids/young adults. I analogize them to Israel. In some ways Israel is a very old country, as in some ways these young people seem to be born with old/mature souls. At the same time Israel as a country is relatively young and can "play and enjoy," celebrate and love.

I saw all of the above in the spirit/laughter and spunk of the IDF gang that we have been honored to share this first few days with. Thank you for Israel. Thank you for protecting all Jewish people all over the world. Thank you for risking your lives. I realized it is the IDF who served before, now and will serve later, that make mom feel safe and free. They make her feel safe for her children and her grandchildren. They make me feel safe! May their spirit, commitment, honor, ability to play and protect be honored by all! "

Part XIII: 2019 Senior Olympics

Chapter 30 Senior Olympic Gold

On August 18, 2019 Sophie Tajch Klisman, age 90, and Lori Klisman Ellis, age 60, competed in the Senior Olympics in Power Walking at Oakland University. We both received gold medals for the 1500M for our age group. In addition we both broke the record for the state of Michigan. Lori beat all the females in all age groups. Sophie walked at a speed of 18.03. Jeff stated if she were to compete in the National Power Walking Olympics with her speed at the age of 90 she would be the fastest in the nation! Way to go mom! She is unstoppable at the age of 90.

Appendix A:
Key Points From Books On The Holocaust

Insight Into Surviving The Concentration Camps
Adapted from "Man's Search for Meaning" by Viktor E. Frankl
Copyright © 1959, 1962, 1984, 1992 by Viktor E. Frankl
Reprinted with permission from Beacon Press, Boston Massachusetts

Dr. Viktor Frankl stated some of the ways he survived various concentration camps in his book *Man's Search for Meaning*. My mother and aunt had many similar ways of survival.

• Having the will to live—It was much easier to die than to continue living.

• Having an instinct for self-preservation—My father snuck out of line when he spotted a mop and bucket and began cleaning in the gas chamber, while the other prisoners from his bunk were poisoned to death and put in the crematorium.

• Having luck—some people say it was pure luck they survived. To survive was purely a miracle. The statistics of surviving was "1 in 28" people in some camps.

• Getting rare instances of human decency—This occurred once when the SS Soldier at Salzwedel gave my mom his sandwich.

• Being optimistic even in the face of doom—My aunt said the war would be over soon when she heard explosions near the concentration camp. It helped her to hang on a little while longer.

• Exhibiting inner freedom even when the outside world was mad—The SS soldiers did whatever they could to dehumanize people. They did not call people by names, but rather called them by the numbers that were tattooed on their arms. The camp robbed people of their dignity by shaving their heads, making everyone wear the same stripped thin clothing. Some prisoners did not have shoes and were forced to stand in the snow for hours. Somehow they dreamt of inner freedom.

• An ability to not give up—Many prisoners committed suicide by being electrocuted on the barbed wire. They did not have perseverance.

• Live life for the future—Nothing could be worse than the camps. They held onto the hope that their lives would be much improved when they could go to America.

- Holding on to loving thoughts of family—Thinking of their beautiful parents and brothers. Thinking about reuniting with their uncle in Uruguay.
- Having hope and positive energy—That was their mantra and the mantra of many Holocaust survivors. Without hope you have nothing.

Dr. Frankl shared he got meaning from life through suffering. If one suffers with Cancer and survives, you may get a new meaning on life. You will appreciate your life more and live it to the fullest. This is also true for those that get an organ transplant from a donor. Another example is that of a Holocaust survivor. The prisoners that survived inhumane and unimaginable conditions had a new meaning of life. They worked hard after the camps, enjoyed their homes, food, their family, etc.

Dr. Frankl shared one cannot prevent suffering but ultimately it is our decision on how we deal with that suffering later on in life. Some people cannot move forward. The lucky ones can find meaning in their suffering and make attempts to keep moving on with their life, in a positive manner. People can still have a beautiful and meaningful life even though they suffered in the past.

My mother and father both found meaning in life after the war in their work, in each other, their children and in their friends. My parents had a positive attitude in life. There were numerous challenges that they faced such as coming to a new country without knowing anyone, not speaking the language, not having any money, and not having their original family. But they worked hard and began to appreciate and enjoy their life in America. They eventually found happiness, laughter, and a satisfying life.

Dr. Frankl helped his patients see a new perspective in their lives. He helped them look into their future, versus dwelling into their past. Many survivors asked "Why did I survive while other family members perished." Many suffered from survivor's guilt. My parents were given a second chance in life, and they chose to live a respectful, kind, loving and nonjudgmental life. They did not seek revenge, or try to instill fear or hatred in me or my brother. They taught us to be respectful, law abiding citizens and strive for a good education. They always told me no one can take your education away from you. No matter what happens in life you will always have your education.

My parents were always proud of my brother's occupation of being a Medical Technologist, and then going back to school to obtain his MSA Degree in Hospital Administration. They too were so thrilled when I obtained my Master's Degree in Speech and Language Pathology. I was impressed with my parent's ability to obtain well respected jobs. They worked hard and won many awards and received many accolades. They saved so that they could pay for our college, provide us with a beautiful home, clothing and food. What a blessing to have them as parents! Growing up we never knew how much they suffered. All we knew was that they loved and protected us.

Having learned that they were survivors (even though we did not know the full meaning of what a survivor was) it brought upon a special parent-child relationship. Both my brother and I never wanted to cause them any aggravation. We wanted to make them proud of us. Although we were not perfect children we aimed to please them, try our best and let them know how much we loved them. I do feel second generation children have a different relationship with their parents in comparison to parents who were not survivors. There is a closeness that is undeniable. It is just so hard to imagine anyone going through all that suffering, especially someone that you love so much.

Dr. Frankl stated the world is still not good but we do not want it to get worse so we must put forth an extreme effort. That is why I am so appreciative of all the Holocaust Memorial Centers around the world and that they are educating and sharing the mantra "Never again." My mother continues at the age of 90 to share her painful story. That is why I wrote the book *4,456 Miles: A Survivor's Search For Closure—Awakening her Daughter's Search for Understanding the Holocaust.* I am thankful for the work my mom and Anne do at the Holocaust Memorial Center. Thank goodness there are videos of survivors sharing their experiences. Thank you to Monnie Must who wrote her *Living Witnesses Faces of the Holocaust.* Thank you to Dr. Charles Silow for creating the powerful *Portraits of Honor.* I hope all 50 states mandate Genocide training.

Let us hope more good will come from these tragedies. I hope one day the world will not use Jewish people as scapegoats for everything that goes wrong in our world. Finally I hope Israel will live in peace and not be targeted in the Middle East. In 2017, there has been a 57% increase in anti-Semitic occurrences just within the United States. Let us deal with this suffering in a positive manner and move forward.

Unfortunately, 2018 and 2019 brought upon an increase in anti-Semitism in Europe and also here in the United States. We experienced a mass shooting in the Tree of Life Synagogue in Pittsburg, White Supremacists and/or Nationalists marched in Charlottesville, Virginia and there has been an increased amount of swastikas appearing on synagogues, tombstones and homes all around the United States. In October, 2019, there was a shooting in Halle, Germany on Yom Kippur, killing two outside of the Synagogue. Thank goodness the doors to the synagogue were locked otherwise it could have been a mass shooting with hundreds of casualties. It appears that the world has not yet learned to accept diversity. That is why we must continue to educate the world about the dangers of being prejudice.

Relating The Holocaust To The Book *When Bad Things Happen to Good People* by Rabbi Harold Kushner

For years I have questioned "Where was G-d during the Holocaust?" How could G-d have allowed such massive killings and tragedy during the Holocaust? That is when I read the book *When Bad Things Happen to Good People*. I re-read the book 15 years later while researching my genealogic roots. Rabbi Kushner asked is it really G-d that causes bad things that happen to us or is it humans?

G-d is powerful and He wants people to get what they deserve in life but He can't always arrange it. He is there to help us and to cope with issues. He stated bad things do happen to good people but we should not blame G-d. G-d does not punish people. G-d does not say you are a bad person and I will punish you. Rabbi Kushner feels it is too difficult of a job even for G-d to keep disorder, disarray and savagery from innocent people. Many innocent people perished in the Holocaust and it was not G-d punishing them for doing anything wrong. Jews were persecuted just because they were not of Aryan decent, and not Catholic.

G-d is there to help you find strength and comfort in life. Some people in the Holocaust lost faith in G-d. Others did not ask G-d why are you doing this to me. Some said see what is happening to the Jewish people, and can you help us. G-d cannot stop malevolent things from happening to people because G-d allows his people to have independence and freedom. If he stopped evil events he would be taking away their freedom. G-d will not intervene to prevent us from doing wrong things or committing harmful acts. G-d may tell us that certain things we do are wrong or harmful and warn us that we will regret our actions. He is hoping we learn from our experiences.

He states being human allows us to cause harm to others and if G-d took away our freedom we would not be human. During the Holocaust G-d looked down on those persecuting the innocent; in shame, sympathy and empathy, because these people have not yet learned how to behave. Once again G-d did not cause the Holocaust but rather human beings such as Adolf Hitler and Otto Adolf Eichmann were the catalyst to cause others to hurt and kill innocent people. G-d noticed how cruel some humans are to others. Was Hitler and other SS Nazis' threatened by others' success and intelligence? Or was it because they needed a scapegoat? Regardless, they chose to perform mass genocide! It still is shocking how they could brainwash so many Germans to perform such inhumane tasks against innocent lives and then go home and try to act normal and assimilate into their family life. Did they go to church and ask for forgiveness or have a conscience?

Dr. Kushner feels it is important to hold on to your faith and that eventually you will be recompensed for all the horrible suffering you endured. Is it possible to forgive and accept a weak and fallible world that disappoints people? Our world can be unfair, cruel, has crime, diseases, accidents and much more. Can you love G-d even if He disappoints you, does not protect you, allows cruelty and terrible things to happen to you?

If my parents stopped believing in G-d what would their life have been like? If they did not have the hope that life would be better inside and outside of the camps what would have happened to them? Miraculously they survived. I wonder if they thought life after the war would still have cruelty and anti-Semitism in it. Somehow, they have learned to love, trust and forgive G-d even though He has limitations. Rabbi Kushner states by understanding that we live in an imperfect world, we can still have a rich and fulfilled life. My parents seem to have followed these beliefs and luckily found a loving spouse, had a wonderful family, and appreciated everything that they worked hard for.

Lori Klisman Ellis

Facts About The Holocaust From The Book *In Broad Daylight: The Secret Procedures Behind The Holocaust By Bullets*

Reprinted with permission from "In Broad Daylight" by Father Patrick Desbois, Arcade Publishing, an imprint of Skyhorse Publishing, Inc.

Even though the locations were all different than where my family members were from in Poland, I thought this was still valuable information to share. After reading *In Broad Daylight: The Secret Procedures behind the Holocaust by Bullets,* by Father Patrick Desbois I learned some horrific, startling and shocking facts about the Holocaust.

1. The German laws stated it was not a crime to kill Jews but it was not ok to steal from Germans who were selling all of the murdered Jewish peoples' possessions. How insane is that. They value the Jew's possessions more than their lives!
2. The mass genocide of the Jews happened during the day, while some of the SS Soldiers encouraged the community to view the killings. I always thought this was a clandestine meeting and no one was allowed to observe!
3. Some deranged police and SS Soldiers forced people to view the crime. The SS Soldiers forced a principal to announce over the loud speaker that students should come outside and view what happens to the Jewish criminals. In reality they were not criminals but ordinary people. I thought being a witness to a crime would obligate you to go to the police and report it, but since the Germans did not consider it a crime to kill Jews, they had no reason to report these horrific events!
4. People have a fascination with watching killings. Just like people have a fascination with observing car accidents.
5. SS Soldiers seem not to care where the killings occur. If there are witnesses to these crimes, that is totally fine. The soldiers do not feel any guilt or remorse for doing mass genocide.
6. The SS Soldiers followed a template which was the same for almost all towns—i.e. they assigned people to be "diggers" and bring their own shovels to dig massive grave sites. They were told exact measurements on how large each grave should be. Many graves held 3,000 bodies or more. Without the SS Soldiers forcing the town's people into assisting, none of this would have been possible.
7. The SS Soldiers assigned people to be "fillers". They had to cover the mass graves with dirt. Sometimes the graves would

still be moving if people were not totally dead upon being shot. These fillers still buried them alive, dead or wounded, and some even took a shovel and knocked them over the head and continued to cover them with dirt. How inhumane was it to witness someone still alive in a mass grave and not assist them in coming out of the grave!

8. They assigned people to be "transporters" and relocate the Jews to the areas where the killings would occur. One transporter had to bring his sleds and transport people without coats or clothing. Many were frozen alive. Then they were lined up in rows, shot, and fell into the massive ditches.

9. The SS Soldiers told prisoners to strip. Take off their clothing, shoes and jewelry. Some were told to bring their valuables with them in a suitcase as a ploy because they thought they were being relocated. In reality they were sent to their death. All valuables were thrown on the ground in piles and then villagers were assigned to transport the valuables of the Jews to a church. Remember according to the Germans it is a crime to take the Jew's valuable items.

10. The SS Soldiers and police assigned people to bring wood/planks to the pit/grave. This was done so Jews would have to line up 5 or 6 in a row on the plank which was draped across the ditch. First they had to undress and wait to be shot. They all fell strategically into the massive ditch and the townspeople had to cover these massive graves with dirt.

11. Many "requisitioned" (people forced to participate in some capacity of the killings of the Jews) were given clothes or shoes that were from the Jews as a thank you for helping. Some people did as commanded while others, on a rare occasion tried to help the Jews if SS Soldiers weren't observing them.

12. Prior to a ghetto being liquidated, many SS Soldiers raped the Jewish woman prior to killing them. Once again, how inhumane is this act!

13. Many residents of cities were forced to be "architects and builders." They had to construct a ghetto using fences and barbed wire.

14. Some SS Soldiers forced Jewish prisoners to perform dances for hours and hours before being killed. The music would be on and no matter what the physical condition of the Jews (disabled, old or young) they were forced to dance for hours or all night. One disabled man who could not walk was strapped

on with rope to his wife's back and forced to dance. This was done to humiliate the Jewish families.

15. The SS Soldiers would be shooting Jews for hours and hours. They requisitioned people to cook for them, or farmers to hand over their milk and other goods so the soldiers could have energy to keep killing. They said it was hard work and they needed their nourishment.

16. Jewish items that were stolen from those that perished such as furniture, clothes, and personal belongings were auctioned off cheaply. People in the town would bring their carts and buy the merchandise. Within 48 hours all reminders of the Jews living in the towns were vanished. Homes were taken over by other residents or the SS Soldiers.

17. It took the participation of residents in every town to do the killings. Without this forced participation none of this would have been possible.

18. Children were curious and often would voluntarily watch. Some climbed on top of a roof and observed. Others came near the ghetto to observe.

19. Teachers were forced to report which children were half Jewish and the students were taken away and murdered. The teachers then continued to teach. These children were forced out from a safe haven. I wonder if the other children in school thought they may be next.

20. Many people had to bury their participation in the Holocaust. I wonder if their part in it haunted them with nightmares for years.

21. I was shocked that many people were willing to tell their story to Father Patrick's team on videotape and recap what they observed so many years ago. Many people felt no remorse. They merely retold their story. On a rare occasion, when the person being videotaped was friendly with their Jewish neighbor and knew them by name, he felt sorrow or pain. The majority of people just thought this was the law and there was nothing wrong in the killing sprees that occurred.

22. I was shocked to hear that the SS Soldiers traveled to parts of Russia, parts of the Ukraine, and not just Germany and Poland to do the mass genocide. They were determined to kill every last Jew alive. I feel if this was not stopped, the Jews in the USA could have been the next target.

23. Some Jewish people were talking and laughing while walking and following the SS soldiers to a new location. This makes me

believe that many did not know they were being transported to their deaths. I wonder if they would have known where they were going (to the massive ditch), would they have revolted and started fleeing?

24. Some Jewish people had to dig their own ditches. Then after digging, they thought they were being rewarded with a break. Loud music was played and they were allowed to sit and rest. Little did they know the ground was detonated with explosives and it went off and killed them instantaneously. Some villagers must have had to get their bodies and place them in the ditch. The SS Soldiers probably realized it was easier for them to continue to line up in rows of 5 or 6 people and shoot them, so they would fall directly in the ditch.

25. Young children were encouraged to sit down at long picnic tables and observe mass shootings. One girl said they killed 5,000 Jews that day. Children were offered candy while they watched the shootings. Father Patrick Desbois stated the SS Soldiers wanted it to appear like a circus.

26. Some villagers were told if they do not perform their tasks they would be killed on the spot. So it was possible that many villagers did not want to obey the laws and felt they did not have any choice.

27. A 16-year-old Jewish girl screamed all night because she was being raped by many German SS Soldiers throughout the night. What kind of sick mentality allows someone to do that to innocent young girls?

28. Villagers were forced to do inhumane jobs such as be a "sanitizer." One man said the graves were so massive, approximately 6 feet deep by 66 feet wide. There was so much blood in them that they forced villagers to find liquid lime because it absorbed the blood from the Jews. This man said that "in the morning it was a butchery and in the evening when the Germans left, the town was cleansed of blood by the Jews." Not one Jew was left!

Father Desbois explained at the end of the book that the Germans were told they had to purify the world by cleansing all the Jews. They were told Jews were evil. Basically they were brainwashed into thinking they were martyrs doing something for the world. Then Father Desbois said even though the Germans thought they were pure and great, they committed evil crimes, like raping Jewish woman, brutally killing children, men and woman and ransacking and stealing their belongings. The Germans were the evil ones. It is hard to believe the German SS Soldiers were so morbidly deranged and inhumane. Once again, they were brainwashed to not see the criminal behaviors in themselves. After massive killings, many nights they were praised for their jobs, thrown parties and provided endless alcohol and given rewards such as cash or beautiful belongings from the Jews. The SS Soldiers often took upscale scarves and clothing and gave them to their girlfriends, even though they were married. There were no repercussions for their criminal behaviors during the war. They were worse than animals and monsters. Did they think this would be acceptable behavior? How was it possible for the world to have gone so crazy?

Many SS Soldiers escaped to South America, changed their identities and carried on with anti-Semitic behavior. Some started underground anti-Semitic groups and enlisted many people and previous soldiers. Some fortunately were hunted down and arrested. Some SS Soldiers killed themselves and many have hidden and gotten away with their crimes.

The Wall street Journal stated "Father Desbois is a generation too late to save lives. Instead, he has saved memory and history." While reading this book, it was impossible to sleep at night. I heard Father Patrick Desbois speak in December, 2018 in Detroit, after being interviewed by Devin Scillian. It was a riveting interview. For Father Desbois and his staff to have interviewed four thousand people must have been heart wrenching. He is on an unbelievable mission to locate mass graves of genocide. He stated he does not leave any markers on these sites because people may attempt to vandalize these spots.

Father Desbois stated what we already know, that genocide is still happening all around the world today. Genocide has occurred in Rwanda, Croatia, Ukraine, Cambodia, Armenia, Indonesia, Serbia, Bangladesh, Albigensian, Irish, Tibetan, Darfur, Libya, Bambini, Kurdish, genocide of Muslims and Croats, and on and on!

Also I want to express an endless amount of gratitude to Father Desbois and his team for creating your organization, Yahad-In Unum and doing your humanitarian work. Please read his exceptional book.

Appendix B: Family Ancestry

The Tree Of Life
Ellis/Klisman Family Tree

A missing part of Lori and her family's life was not knowing names of people in her family. She was missing her "Family Tree." The tree of life was chopped down to the stump. After much research on Ancestry.com, Jewishgen.org and hiring a Genealogist, her tree is blooming with new leaves and flowers. It has been resurrected and by sharing names of family and information about them, Lori and her family are watering their tree, watching it bloom, and keeping the memory of those that perished alive. There is a how-to guide on growing your own tree, doing DNA research, and watching your family grow!

Liba Rozrazowska's Pedigree Tree

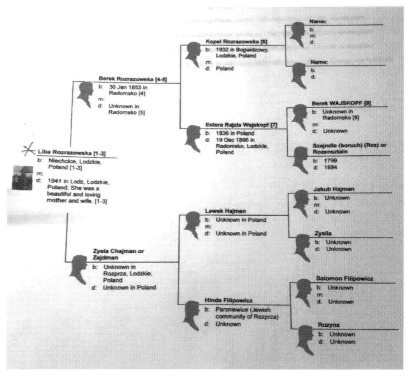

Icek Berek's Pedigree Tree

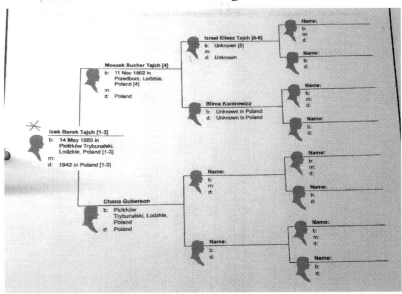

Zysla Tajch/Sophie Klisman's Pedigree Tree

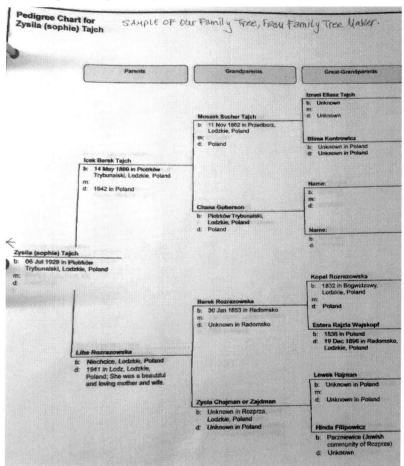

4,456 Miles

Lori Klisman Ellis's Pedigree Tree

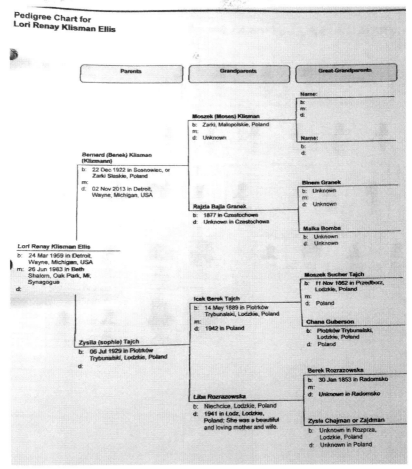

207

Sample of the Ellis/Klisman Family Tree from Ancestry.com

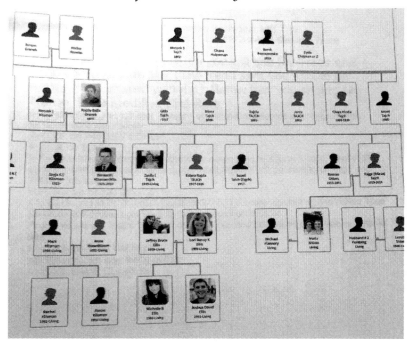

Sharing tree information with other friends and/or family members from Davya Cohen.

1- Go to ancestry.com.
2- Click on Trees on the black ancestry bar (upper left)
3- Scroll down to bottom of that list- Click on Create & Manage Trees
4- Your Ellis tree should be there -
Across the top of the screen you will see My Trees and Trees Shared with Me. (The tree I sent you should be under trees shared with me). Below that you should see Name, Date Modified and Role
5- Under Role you will see Owner - under owner you will see Invite Family
6- Click on Invite Family
7- Click on INVITE PEOPLE
8- Click on EMAIL
9- Fill in email and make sure the drop down next to it says Guest. I NEVER give anyone permission to be a EDITOR as they will be able to change and modify the tree.
10- Click on SEND INVITE
11- Click on I'M FINISHED SENDING INVITES new screen opens called Tree Settings if it doesn't go back to the previous screen
Right above the black box that says EMAIL and shows an envelope is another box.
11- Click on Tree Settings
12- Check Can see living people
13 Click SAVE CHANGES

The Family Tree

How does one find out about their family tree when the majority of their family had been murdered in the Holocaust? That was the question. I began with Ancestry.com. I remembered my father's caregiver, Stash, saying he did an online search from another site called Heritage.com where he found an uncle and several other family members he did not know he had. So I thought I would do a search as well.

It was quite simple to get started. On Ancestry.com there is a green rectangular box that says "Start a free trial" and there is a brownish-orange rectangular box that says "See How it's Done." I started the free family tree by putting in family names beginning with my immediate family. Then I interviewed my mother for her siblings' names and places of birth and the family tree continued to grow.

The site showed green leaves on the tree which meant there were possible hints that may be relatives. Clicking on the leaves and reading the information provides additional information and possible matches. Sometimes, it may not be a match. Ancestry.com is affiliated with Stanley Diamond's project of JRI-Poland (Jewish Record Indexing-Poland) so there is a wealth of information his volunteers put into this from their searches on the Holocaust.

Also, I hired a genealogist from my mother's hometown named is Jacek Bednarek. His email address is: bednajac@poczta.onet.pl Not only did he search the town of Piotrkow, but he also went into Lodz where my mother's family relocated to. He said he could do research in several towns in Poland. He was reasonable for the amount of work he put into it. Also, how can you put a price tag on family? It was well worth the $200.00 I spent. He hit the jackpot for me with grandparent names, great grandparent names and he said he could keep going. The difficulty was that my mother did not know who these family members were and because she was so young she did not recognize the names. The beauty of hiring this genealogist was that he ascertained all the records from:

- Documents of the city of Piotrkow: in the books of impermanent resident of Piotrkow. He stated my family had roots in Przedborz.
- He found the list of students of elementary schools in Piotrkow.
- Jacek found the documents of the city of Przedborz: the books of residents of that town.

- The documents of the county of Piotrkow: the list of recruits, the budgets of the Jewish Community of Piotrkow.
- The metrical books of the Jewish community of Piotrkow.
- The documents of the Jewish Berek Joselewicz elementary school.
- The Passport applications from 1926-1929. Izrael Tajch, the brother of Icek Berek Tajch moved to Uruguay in 1930 or later.

This is just some of the information I found on my family tree:
My mother Zysla Tajch (Sophie Klisman) had four siblings: Estera Rajzla Tajch who was born in 1917 and unfortunately passed away in 1926. To our surprise her birth date matched my mother's one brother: Izrael Teich. Note the difference in spelling. For some reason all the documents showed this discrepancy. He too was born on May 17, 1917. My mother never knew there were twins in the family. Her sister that survived the camp with her was Fajga Tajch (Felicia Shloss). We found out her true date of birth was different than what we had originally believed. Her brother Moszek Tajch was born in 1922 and perished in 1941. These dates confirmed the information I found out several months ago from the Memory project.

Her father was Icek Berek Tajch, born in 1899 and perished in 1942. Also, Jacek found out his height, weight, and additional health related information on him. He was not a tall man, which explains my mother's petite stature. His wife, my grandmother, was Liba Rozrazozowska who was born in 1888 and perished in 1941.

Liba had one sister named Szajndla Rozrazowska. She was married to Zelik Bialowas. They had two daughters. Szajndla and Zelik got a divorce, which was highly unusual back then and the three of them moved to Paris. No one knows what happened to them.

Liba's parents were Zysla Hajman and Berek Rozrazowska. How history repeats itself, as my mother was named after her grandmother (both Zysla) and coincidently my father Bernard had the same Polish name Berek. I was told there were only a few names and people were named the same names over and over again. Also, I went to a seminar prior to going to Poland and Professor Ziv from U-M shared that the name Green was popular, so the Jews tried to individualize their names—one family was Greenbaum, one was Greenberg, and one was Greenspaun, etc.

Zysla's parents were Hinda Filipowicz and her father was Lewek Hajman.

Berek Rozrazowska's parents were Estera Rajzla Wajskopf and his father's name was Kopel Rozrazowska.

There is also information on Icek Berek Tajch's siblings. Icek had four sisters named Blima, Rajzla, Jenta, Chaja Hinda, and one brother Izrael. Izrael Tajch was married to Gitle M. Milsztejn and received a fairly big dowry. Lucky for them they took the money and moved to Uruguay. They escaped the Holocaust. Blima was born in 1886 and was married. Rajla was born in 1891 and was married to Jakob Wolf Brygier. Jenta was born in 1902 and Chaja Hinda was born in 1903. Izrael was born in 1905.

I have not done much research yet on my father Berek Klizman/ Bernard Klisman. What I do know is that he had seven siblings: six brothers and one sister. His family consisted of his father Moishe, his mother Rajzla, his twin younger brothers Chaskiel and Szyja, his older brothers Jakob, Leon, Icek Majer and Pincha. He had a sister Luba. His sister was married and had a baby boy. No one knows if the boy survived. Rumors were that they may have given the son away to a family with the hopes of him surviving. Unfortunately we do not know his last name. Leon was in a prison in Russia during the time of the Holocaust because the prison guard thought he was a spy since he was wearing a nice warm coat. Jakob helped to bribe the guard with Vodka to get his brother out. Jakob and Leon and my father were reunited after the war.

Documents that Jacek found stated that they had immigration papers with "Bolivia" stamped on it. The dream was to leave and be together in Bolivia. Unfortunately, they were not able to go. My dad's two brothers: Leon and Jakob Klisman went to Melbourne, Australia. Leon married Lisa and never had children. She was a nurse in Germany and they met, fell in love, and moved to Australia together. Jakob, the oldest brother, met Karola and got married and had one son Mori Klisman. Mori was a Psychologist and helped patients in the outback. He was not close with his family. Occasionally we kept in touch through the internet. Mori got married and had two children. I along with my brother Mark and Mom were fortunate enough to meet our two uncles when they came to Michigan for a visit. My parents did visit them once in Melbourne, Australia.

My dad, Bernard came to the United States of America all alone. He made it to New York and then to Michigan. My father had twins on his side of the family as well. I did a search on Ancestry.com and it appears that my dad's twin siblings were Szyja and Chaskiel Klisman. Their names were spelled Klizman and other times it was spelled Klizmann. They were both born on July 6, 1925. Unfortunately they did not survive the camps. The twins were arrested on May 22, 1942 when they were 17 and sent to the ghetto in Sosnowiec. They were transported to Auschwitz. From there they may have gone to Kochendorf not far from Heilbronn. Next they were sent to Ulm, Dachau. Records indicated Chaskiel perished in February 18, 1945 possibly on the death march; while Szyja died March 20, 1945 (A month later) in Zwieselberg, Baden-Wurttemberg, German when he was only 19 years old.

My father's parents were Moszek Klisman and Rajzla Bajla Granek. My father was very close with his mother. I recall when I was in my teens, I heard my uncle had a photo of his mother. I asked my Uncle Leon to send it to me so I could make a copy. I copied and enlarged the photo and framed it for my father. Little did I know that was the best gift he ever received! He hung it up in his bedroom. That was the only family photo he had. Unfortunately I do not have any information on Icek Majer or Pincha.

The wonderful thing about Ancestry.com was that I was able to get detailed information about several family members. On Moszek Tajch I received this memo "Does the Moszek Tajch in this record match the person in your tree?"

It said the following:
Ghetto: Lodz
Name: Moszek Tajch
Gender: Male
Birthdate: 1922
Profession: Schaftelmacher (Upper Shoe Maker)
Address: 13 Flat 1 Reiter Strasse
Residence: Lodz, Poland
Death Date: 7 Sep 1941
Death Place: Lodz ghetto

It was a match! On the bottom, it said "If you click yes this information will be sent to your tree." How exciting that it does a lot of work for you. Another search on him said "photo: yes." This is when I contacted the Holocaust Memorial Center in Washington D.C. and miraculously they had a photo of him.

On that same search it stated father: Icek Berek, Mother: Liba Rozanowska (I noticed often times spellings of names differed from document to document. Most spellings were Rozrazowska. Another search on Ancestry.com for my Uncle Jakob (that passed away) provided me with his burial registry (JOWBR: Jewish Online Worldwide Burial Registry). Much to my surprise it gave me his Hebrew name, his birth date, his birth place, the death date, his burial date, his burial plot, burial place, his father's name and mother's name as well as the cemetery.

Also, people have gone on Ancestry.com and other sites affiliated with JRI-Poland searching for DNA information. It is so unbelievable what information is available when one starts searching.

Once the family tree is started you can share this information with other members of your family by sending them an invitation to come to your tree. You have the option to make the tree private or public. To my surprise I know have over 1500 relatives on the tree titled "Ellis/Klisman Family Tree." It's unbelievable to me because I always felt I had a small family.

This book includes information on several family members. Or you can go to my Ancestry.com family tree and read their "Life Story," "Facts" and view their photo "Gallery" there. Be prepared, once you get on this site it is addicting. It is hard to walk away from this wealth of information.

Family Stories

Legend has it or shall I say Aunt Felicia used to share the story of her great grandmother Fiega Kzrck Shock. Supposedly she lived until 116 years of age and died during World War I. She supposedly owned land. She was on the Tajch side of the family. Unfortunately my research cannot validate this information. Wouldn't it be wonderful to have such longevity in the family?

Another story on my husband Jeff Ellis' side of the family goes as follows: Jeff's grandfather "Poppy" came to the USA all alone from Russia when he was only 13 years old. He wanted to be a cowboy and that is why he came here. Fortunately for him, he escaped the violence in Europe. Poppy's grandfather was the body guard to Czar Nicholas in Russia. He was told to walk as far as he could and that would become his land. He grew potatoes which was used in making vodka. He must have been a big, strong and healthy guy to have been a body guard, just like Jeff. Jeff competes in the Senior Olympics in Weight Lifting. He has won 17 gold medals, one bronze and one silver medal and is still going strong.

Jeff Ellis' father was Robert (Bob) Ellis. He was a Corporal in the 30th Infantry Division, U.S. Army. He was in the "Battle of the Bulge." His job was carrying a 40 pound radio pack while trying to get rid of or "expel" the Germans. Bob won a bronze Star!

My mother, Sophie Klisman, became an international speaker on the Holocaust. This brave young girl who survived the Lodz ghetto and three concentration camps had the courage 74 years later to start sharing her story at the Holocaust Center in Farmington Hills, Michigan and then continued on this heroic mission to share her story in Poland and Israel.

Bernard Klisman, Felicia and Roman Shloss were strong, heroic survivors of the Holocaust. Felicia also was brave and courageous in sharing her story to young people at the Holocaust Memorial Center in both Michigan and Florida.

Resources From *It's All Relative* By A.J. Jacobs And From Lori Ellis

Reproduced with permission from "It's All Relative" by A.J. Jacobs, copyright 2017 by Simon and Schuster

There are also many wonderful books on genealogy:
- *Jewish Roots in Poland*
- *Where Once We Walked: A Guide to the Jewish Communities Destroyed in the Holocaust*
- *Jewish Roots in Ukraine*
- *Jewish Roots in Moldova*

Interesting websites you may want to explore are:
- CyndisList.com
- Archives.com
- GenealogyBank.com
- FindAGrave.com
- LibertyEllisFoundation.org
- https://ChroniclingAmerica.loc.gov/

When pursuing your own family tree there are many useful resources such as:
- Ancestry.com
- MyHeritage.com
- FamilySearch.com
- FindMyPast.com
- Famicity - available on Google Play or the App Store
- SmartDraw.com

To connect with relatives all over the world you may want to use:
- Geni.com
- Wikitree.com
- Skype
- Facebook

There are also numerous DNA tests that you may want to pursue such as:
- AncestryDNA
- 23andme.com
- FamilyTreeDNA.com
- Living DNA
- AfricanAncestry.com

- MyHeritage.com/dna
- HomeDNA.com
- GPSOrigins.com
- ORIG3N.com

There are just a few newspapers that contain valuable DNA information such as:
- Newspapers.com
- Ancestry.com - newspapers: https://www.ancestry.com/search/categories/38/

There are sites to research based on one's ethnicity such as:
- JewishGen.org
- WieWasWie.nl (Dutch)
- Kirchenbuchportal.de (German)

If you are interested in researching birth/death/marriage certificates you may want to explore:
- Ancestry.com
- USVital records.org/Birth/Certificates
- Archives.com
- Get.birthcertificatestate.com/Order-Birth/Certificate
- Findagrave.com
- Fold3.com
- JewishGen.org

Appendix C:
DNA Information

Let me start by saying thank goodness I did not marry my cousin. With that being said many Jewish people with ancestors in Europe have found out they are married to i.e. a sixth cousin. I heard this is not really marrying family. I learned a new term today: Endogamy. Endogamy means Jewish people stayed in a limited geographic area. Most people married within their own culture and even some married within their own family. This may sound like inbreeding to some, but this is what happened in the small communities in Eastern Europe (Poland) as well as many other areas. No one had cars and so it was hard to meet other possible suitors in different cities or communities. They ended up falling in love with other people in their same culture, relatives or distant cousins. I probably share enough DNA with thousands of people for Ancestry to think we are cousins, but they may not be blood related. I reproduced cells from related people and this must be why I have 1000+ cousins. It appears that I share much more DNA with other Jewish families.

There is no surprise on my end that I am 100% European Jewish. I was surprised that I did not see my first cousins on my tree or second cousins, but then I found out that Loretta Stone Feinberg used the Heritage DNA test and perhaps Sam used a different DNA test as well. There is a way to link it all, and I am currently exploring GEDmatch.

I am starting to reach out to some possible third cousins with high probability for a match. Ancestry displays a green bar which may say you have a moderate match or high probability or low probability. You can click on the name of your match and then click on the little "i" in the greyish brown circle for additional information. There is a chart available called DNA Detectives Autosomal Statistics which indicates your centimorgans or cM and then it shares with you your relationship to them. For example, 900 cM indicates a first cousin, while 3,600 cM indicates a parent-child relationship. Sounds easy to follow, right? However this is not accurate for Jews after their second cousins. This is because our DNA is shared with many shared ancestors in many different parts of our tree. For additional information read the article listed on the next page.

Ancestry tests such as 23andme or MyHeritage share segment length. Look for people who share at least a single segment in the 20-30 cM or greater as well as at least 10-15 cM + range.

Information was taken from an online article called *No, You Don't Really Have 7,900 4th Cousins: Some DNA Basics for Those with Jewish Heritage.* It's on the Medium App. The author of the article was Jennifer Mendelsohn.
https://medium.com/@CleverTitleTK/no-you-dont-really-have-7-900-4th-cousins-some-dna-basics-for-those-with-jewosh-heritage-857f873399ff

DNA Research

Do you need a degree in Genetic Genealogy to get answers? Well it certainly would be easier to understand one's DNA. Where does one begin getting answers? I am a novice in this area, but from my experience start with spitting into a test tube. I personally used the ancestry kit because I was too chicken to use 23 and Me. 23 and Me is twofold. First it tells you your genealogy information such as you are 100% Ashkenazi Jew and secondly it tells you your medical information. i.e. you may have a gene to make you more at risk for Alzheimer's or Parkinson's disease. Of course you could keep this information unopened. For me personally I would ask my husband to look at the results and not tell me. Then I would think, if he did not tell me, it was bad news and I will get Alzheimer's disease. I would worry myself sick. If I had the gene it would not necessarily mean I would get the disease, but deep down I would think I would since my father and uncle had it. Anyways, there is FamilyTree DNA, MyHeritage, Living DNA and more.

After you spit into a test tube, you wait and wait and wait. Approximately 6 weeks later the results of my DNA test were emailed to me. I went on Ancestry.com and clicked the link that said DNA and no surprise to me I found I was 100% Eastern European Jewish. The big surprise was that it said I had 1000+ cousins. Some were third cousins and many fourth, and some fourth to sixth cousins. With Jewish ancestry, often times there are more matches which are due to endogamy. Results may indicate someone is a third cousin but in reality they may be a fifth cousin. That is why it is important to look specifically at one's DNA.

After hearing of the 1,000+ matches I was not about to start contacting each and every possible family member. The few select ones I did were receptive to me contacting them, but we struggled with finding out how we were connected to each other. Ancestry does list names of relatives that we share, but none of those names were on my family tree or on the other person's tree. So where do they fit in to our tree? My analogy to the tree is working on a puzzle. You can spend hours and hours to find a match or see where the piece fits or you may not find the match.

Being frustrated I looked into DNA a bit more. I discovered GEDmatch.com. GEDmatch is an internet site that has volunteer Genetic Genealogists that analyze your DNA that you sent them and come up with a list of other people who may have matching DNA. Initially I had to download my ancestry DNA (Unopened, or as a zip file. Do not open that zip file because it will not work). Once downloaded, you then proceed to upload it to GEDmatch. Once again, you need to be patient and wait for the whole file to be processed. Once you get the message "done" you have to wait 24-48 hours for the volunteers to go through this information, share it on their site and find others with possible similar DNA. Basically "GEDmatch is a third party website for analysis and comparisons of raw autosomal DNA data from genetic genealogy testing companies."

This site helps to identify cousins who were tested on other genealogical sites. If I did not upload this file to GEDmatch, my DNA would only be matched to other participants who did Ancestry.com testing. I would be lacking valuable information if I did not pursue further information.

I strongly recommend going to GEDmatch.com (or now called Genesis) and listening to training videos for more information on DNA. If you are not Jewish you only need to match 7 cM (Centimorgans). However if you are Jewish, GEDmatch prefers that you have 23 cM and match 4-5 additional matching segments of at least <8 cMs. For more specific information on DNA refer to the article on GEDmatch called DNA Adoption, "Those with Ashkenazi Jewish descent will need to make some adjustments to the process." Anyone more distant than a third cousin is often very difficult to find.

So my hope is to continue on my quest to find new relatives and learn about old relatives. It is so exciting to receive emails that say "We are a DNA match on the ____ chromosome, or we may be family." I hope my family eventually does DNA testing as well and continues finding more family. I now have a passion to continue learning about genealogy and searching the web for more information. In addition, I hope to one day find photos of my lost family. If that is not possible, I hope we continue talking about family and searching for more family.

Once again, Book 2 "Ellis/Klisman Family Tree" is available or could be viewed on Ancestry.com. This contains a family's profile, facts, a gallery of photos, and also allows you to add to the tree.

This is a sample of the 1,000 plus people who may be relatives. Due diligence has to be completed, such as checking their DNA results.

Appendix D:
Creating Your Own Trip To Poland
Poland Itinerary for the Ellis/Klisman Family

Day #1 Fly to Warsaw Thursday evening—Thursday, July 7th
- Air Canada out of Detroit 6:35 to Toronto at 7:39.
- Leave Toronto at 9:55—arrive 12:20 the next day.
  Expedia Itinerary
  Bring Passport and License
  Flight #

Day # 2 Check into the hotel Friday. Friday, 7/8/2016—Warsaw
- Hotel: Hampton by Hilton Warsaw City Centre. Close to Warsaw Jewish Square. 25 minutes from the airport. Taxi drive to Warsaw Jewish Square and walk to Train Station. Breakfast buffet included—Ul. Wspolna 72, Warsaw 00687
  Tel: + 48-22317-2700
  Confirmation—July 8–10th
- Chabad house—dinner—make arrangements in advance
  Or Shabbat service @ Beit Warszawa Synagogue. Saturday. Wiertnicza 113 +48 695 519 444.
- Beit Warszawa, the progressive congregation in Warsaw. They can tell us about Judaism alive in Poland. Dinner.
- Chopin Concert?
- Ask concierge about tickets to Museum of History of Polin Jews—need 5 tickets for July 9 around 3:00

Day #3 Warsaw—Saturday 7/9/2016—Warsaw
- Breakfast buffet included.
- Jewish Heritage Tour—Leaves every hour
  Possibly 9:00–1:00
  Pick up at hotel
- Nozyk Synagogue, the Warsaw ghetto, Umshlagpalt—monument and wall. Ghetto walk.
- Panoramic tour of Old Town Square and Lazienki Park
- The Jewish Resistance Bunker at Mila 18—a stone in honor of the Jewish underground who died on Mila Street # 18
- The Stawski street buildings—where the SS had their headquarters

4,456 Miles

- Gensa Cemetery—graves of 250,000 people, largest cemetery in Poland
- Lunch
- Afternoon: Museum of history of Polish Jews—it faces the Warsaw ghetto. Muzeum Histori Żydów Polskich, Mordechaja Anielewicza 6 street, 00–157 Warszawa, +48 22 471 03 01Poland. Get tickets in advance—closed on Tuesday! It takes 2–3 hours. Phone +48 22 471 03 01
- Stay over another night in Hampton by Hilton Warsaw City Centre.
- Eat breakfast buffet—included, check out of hotel, and head to Lodz by 8:30
- Warsaw to Lodz, Poland. Distance between Warsaw and Lodz is 118 kilometers and 799.99 meters. Warsaw is 73.8 miles away from Lodz. 129.58 km / 80.52 mile—1 hour 30 minutes

Day #4 Lodz—Sunday 7/10/2016
- Eat breakfast buffet—included, check out of hotel, and head to Lodz by 8:15
- Meet driver and Leave Warsaw and go to Lodz at 8:15.
- If time permits check bags in behind desk, at Novotel Centrum Hotel. Room will not be ready until 2:00. Or we can keep luggage in van. Al.Pilsudskiego 11a
Itinerary for each part of the trip
- Go to New Lodz Cemetery @ 11:00 a.m. It is on Ul. Bracka and Ul. Zmienna. Service for Tajch family—part of Lodz ghetto—explore the rest of the ghetto. Location for Liba Tajch is U-VI Row: 5 Grave 480 Side L, Location for Moszek is CZ-VI Row 6 Grave 410 Side L
- The Rabbi in Lodz is Symcha Keller. +48 42 632 04 27 Symcha@jewishcommunity.org.pl He will meet us there. Closed on Saturday.
- Have guide take us to the following areas:
  - Ghetto Litzmannstadt:
  - Go to homes: Prusa 12 in the ghetto, by Piekarska—Tajch's home
  - Reiter Strasse 13, Flat 1—now it is Urzednicza. Another home in the ghetto
- See the Bridges in the ghetto.
- Is there still a Pdeiffergasse 12? Liba lived there! It does not show up on Google Earth
- Visit mom's school—#9 B Ulica—it's gone—now it is Rybna 15,

new street name Fischstrasse. After the school it housed the Russian Jews and then became a slipper store.
- See the Lagiewniki Park in Lodz where Alshtot Synagogue used to be—may need tickets
- Reicher Synagogue is still open. Ul.Rewolucji. 1905 r. 28
- Radegast Station—Independence Traditions Museum in Lodz

Day # 5 in Lodz—Monday July 11
- Karol Poznanski palace.
- Piotrkowska Street—check out the architecture of buildings
- Manufaktura shopping center
- Tour of city
- If not enough to do we can head over to Piotrkow early and then come back to Lodz
- Stay over again in Novotel Centrum Hotel in Lodz
- Leave Lodz at 9:00 a.m. Piotrkow is 16 miles south of Lodz.

Day # 6 to Piotrkow/Trybunalski—Morning, Tuesday July 12
- See old town Square—renovated
- Berek and family lived at Slowaki St 67. Kaliska st 57 is the former Slowacki Street 67. Now it is a big house.
- Berek and family also lived at Sieradzka 8.
- The Stanislaw Staszic Jewish Boy's School was at Pilsudski Street—now Wojska Polskiego 9. This was Izrael's school.
- Mom's school in second grade was Berek Joselewicz Jewish Elementary School. It was close to the city park at Aleja 3 Maja Street. Probably 28 or 30.
- Great Synagogue on Jerozolimska st. It's a library now.
- Leave Lodz around 1:00 p.m. and drive 1 hour and 42 minutes to Sosnowiec without traffic—with traffic 2 hours 36 minutes.

Day # 6 Sosnowiec, by Katowice—Afternoon, Tuesday July 12
- Dad and Moris' School: Wesole Przedskole School or Ostrogorska 21.
- Jewish cemetery—Milowice—Ul. Stralowa and B. Prusa. Look for dad's parents—Moses Klisman and Raizel Granek.
- House: Prodsusk 42. This does not show up on Google Earth.
- Plaque of Sosnowitz Dulag School. Plaque commemorates the 1993 in memory of the Holocaust victims.
- The site of the former Great Synagogue.
- View the Jewish Cemetery of Gospodarcza Street—closed on weekends.

- The Jewish cemetery of Pastewna Street.
- The memorial in the area of the former ghetto
- The monument in honor of the victims of the Holocaust and the camp in the schoen factory.
- Leave Sosnowiec in evening and drive one hour to Krakow.
- Stay over at the Hotel Ester
  Hotel: http://hotel-ester.krakow.pl
  Confirmation—3 rooms & 1 room
  Szeroka 20 Krakow, Lesser Poland
  +48 12 429 11 88

Day # 7 Krakow—Wednesday July 13—Auschwitz
- Auschwitz -Birkenau Museum and Memorial Guided Tour from Krakow Afternoon tour. Discover Cracow. Contact +48 12 357 21 70. Call to verify pick up spot at our hotel. Only bring in small bags 30 x 20 x 10 cm.
  1 hour 9 minutes each way from Krakow.
  Tour: Viator
  Booking reference
- Galicia Museum or eat in Jewish Restaurant by Kazimierz

Day # 8 Krakow—Thursday July 14—Zakopane
- Private tour to Zakopane and Tatra Mountains Day Trip from Krakow. Itinerary. 9 hour tour. Confirm pick up in advance. Ask for pick up at Hotel Ester. 2 hours each way.
  Tour: Viator
- Stay overnight again in Hotel Ester.
- Check out of hotel. Have breakfast and sight see all day in Krakow and then head back to Warsaw. (4 hour drive)

Day # 9 Sightsee in Krakow then head back to Warsaw—Friday July 15
- Tour guide Krakow Bus #1 Aneta Rypysc Tel: +48-602-710-733 recommended by Elaine at Temple Israel. Or Walking Tour –3 hours of city.
- Kazimierez—Jewish section—We will see the Old Synagogue, a massive fortress-like building erected in the 15th and 16th centuries, the "Temple" and the Remuh synagogue. We will continue to the little museum at the Drug store inside the Jewish ghetto, and Schindler's Factory.
- Miodowa street cemetery, which is still in use with its ornate monuments.

- Go to Jewish book store Jarden in the Jewish Quarter of Krakow. Lucy Les is the owner. Store is adjacent to the kosher restaurants and just a walk from the hotel in Kazimierz. Her email is jarden@jarden.pl
  Phone +48 504 044 794. She was helpful in private tours.
- Leave Krakow around 5:00 and 4 hour drive to Warsaw.
- Check luggage in Hampton by Hilton Warsaw Airport Hotel at 17 Stycznia 39 F street, Warsaw. Confirmation—2 rooms with sofa in one room.
  Phone number +48 222041800

Day # 10 Check out of Hotel and leave. Saturday July 16th.
- They provide a boxed breakfast to go.
- Check out of hotel and go to Airport. Free shuttles to the airport. Fly home.
  Flight information: Flight leaves Warsaw at 11:55 a.m. Polish airlines and arrives in Chicago at 2:35 p.m.. Leaves Chicago at 6:48 p.m. and arrives in Detroit at 9:19 p.m.

Things to do before the trip:
- Get Polish money from Bank
- Order birth certificates for mom's family in advance if she still wants it and pick up in Piotrkow.
- Purchase Polanski museum tickets in advance
- Purchase museum of Polin tickets in advance
- Contact credit card that we will be out of the country
- Go to ATT and get plan for out of country for one month for phone.
- Bring memorial candles, pebbles for cemetery, yarmulkes
- Bring plug sockets for Poland 230V 50 hz AC. 2 round pin sockets.

Travel Tips

Lucy Les is the owner of the Jewish Book Store, Jarden, in the Jewish Quarter of Krakow. Through her my friend made arrangements for a private driver with a van (for the entire day) from Sosnowiec to Chrzanow and back to the Krakow train station. She and her husband were very helpful with navigation assistance. Their bookstore is located adjacent to the kosher restaurants and just a walk from the hotel we stayed in Kazimierz.

Website: http://jarden.pl/page.php?t=about_us
Her email: Jarden@jarden.pl
Phone: +48 504 044 794

It is less expensive to take a train from Warsaw to Krakow.
There are very comfortable and fast trains available. Trip takes 2.5 hours. It is easy to buy tickets online http://intercity.pl/en/ .

Driver would take about 1400 PLN and trip would last about 4.5–5 hours

Great travel site: www.inyourpocket.com
You can search by country or city and it has lots of helpful information. You should definitely take the time to check this site.

Sampling Of Sites

Here are some sites I researched before traveling to Poland

Restaurant Tipping:
http://www.inyourpocket.com/poland/Tipping-Tribulations_72657f

Water in Restaurants:
http://www.inyourpocket.com/poland/krakow/basics/Water

Public Toilets:
http://www.inyourpocket.com/poland/krakow/basics/Toilets

Taxis:
http://www.inyourpocket.com/poland/warsaw/travel-info/taxis
http://www.inyourpocket.com/poland/krakow/arrival-transport/Taxis

Hotels

Hampton by Hilton Warsaw City Centre
Tel: +48-22317-2700
ul. Wspolna 72, Warsaw, 00687

This hotel in Warsaw was about 25 minutes from airport, taxi drive to Warsaw Jewish Square and you can walk to the train station. We stayed here on first day. Boutique style, with very clean rooms with an amazing breakfast buffet which was included in the price.

Hotel Eden
Tel: +48-12430-6565/Mobile:+48-606-385-386
5 Ciemna Street, 31-053 Krakow
eden@hoteleden.pl

This hotel in Krakow is in the heart of the Jewish Quarter of Kazimierz. Great location for touring. We stayed here for a few nights. Quaint, very clean, kosher breakfast included and the only mikvah in the area.

Ibis Krakow Stare Miasto Hotel
Tel: +48-12355-2900/1-800-221-4542
ul. Pawia 15, Krakow 31154
h7161@accor.com

This hotel in Krakow is outside of the Jewish quarter of Kazimierz, not located on a main street but close. We did not stay at this hotel but know others that have.

Hampton by Hilton Warsaw Airport
Tel: +48-22204-1800
17 Stycznia 39F Street, Warsaw, 02148

This hotel in Warsaw was close to airport. Was convenient for an early morning complimentary hotel shuttle to the airport. We stayed here on the last day. Ate dinner at their onsite restaurant and they provided boxed breakfasts to go.

The websites listed were active as of December 2019 and are subject to change.

Appendix E: Photo Gallery

Early Photos

Sophie in the Displaced Persons camp in Germany

Sophie in the Displaced Persons camp in Germany

4,456 Miles

Sophie in the Displaced Persons camp in Germany

Additional photos of Sophie prior to coming to USA.

4,456 Miles

This was Sophie's first dress made from a curtain or a table cloth, by the headmaster in the DP camp in Germany. Sophie was approximately 16 years old in this photo.

Bernard and Sophie Klisman shortly after they were married.

4,456 Miles

Family Photos

My beautiful parents: Sophie and Bernard Klisman

Sophie and Bernard's children: Lori Klisman Ellis and Mark Klisman. Photo was taken at their grandson Joshua Ellis' Bar Mitzvah. 2004

4,456 Miles

Sophie and Bernard at their granddaughter, Michelle Ellis' Bat Mitzvah. The front row are Bernard and Sophie Klisman, their daughter Lori and her husband Jeff Ellis. All the grandkids are in this photo: In the middle row are Aaron Klisman on the far left, Joshua Ellis is in the middle, and Rachel Klisman on the right. In the back row are Mark Klisman, Sophie and Bernard's son, the Bat Mitzvah girl Michelle Ellis and Mark's wife, Anne Klisman. 2001

Another photo at Sophie and Bernard's granddaughter Michelle's Bat Mitzvah. In the front row from left to right is Bernard and Sophie Klisman, Sophie's sister Felicia Shloss, Felicia's daughter Marla, Marla's daughter Elizabeth and Felicia and Roman's other daughter Loretta Stone Feinberg. In the back row from left to right is Roman Shloss (Felicia's husband), Lori Ellis, Lori and Jeff's children Joshua and Michelle Ellis, Lori's husband Jeff Ellis and Elizabeth's father Michael Flannery. 2001

Bernard and Sophie Klisman's four grandchildren. From left to right: Rachel Klisman, Michelle Ellis, Joshua Ellis and Aaron Klisman. The photo was taken at Michelle's Bat Mitzvah. 2001

4,456 Miles

Sophie and Bernard Klisman's grandson, Joshua Ellis' Bar Mitzvah.
Back row: Jeff Ellis and Mark Klisman
Middle row: Michelle Ellis, Joshua Ellis, Lori Ellis, Anne Klisman, Aaron Klisman and Rachel Klisman
Front row: Bernard and Sophie Klisman

This photo was taken on June 30, 2018 at their grandson Joshua Ellis' wedding. From left to right: Benny Ebert-Zavos and Rachel Klisman. Anne Klisman, Michelle Ellis. Bride is Kelsey Prena-Ellis. Sophie Klisman. Groom is Joshua Ellis. Joshua's parents Lori and Jeff Ellis. Aaron Klisman and Mark Klisman.

Sophie Klisman, as featured in the book Living Witnesses—Faces of the Holocaust *by Monni Must. 2009*

FIDF Photos From The 2019 Mission

An IDF woman soldier, Major General Klifi, Gita Mann a Holocaust survivor, Sophie Tajch Klisman a Holocaust survivor, the President of the FIDF, Col. (Res) Atar Daga, and another IDF soldier on the 2019 FIDF mission.

The IDF soldiers with the FIDF Delegation, along with Gita and Sophie in the Buczyna forest in Poland where 800 innocent Jewish children were murdered.

The IDF soldiers in Buczyna forest with Sophie Tajch Klisman.

4,456 Miles

Sophie Tajch Klisman and Gita Mann marching with the IDF soldiers and FIDF Delegation in Auschwitz-Birkenau Concentration Camp and Extermination Camp.

Sophie and Gita shared their stories of survival. It was a misrable, cold, rainy day in Auschwitz-Birkenau Concentration and Extermination Camp.

Lori Klisman Ellis

Gita Mann on the left, Sophie Tajch Klisman in the middle and Anne Klisman on the right; lighting candles for those that were murdered.

Sophie enjoying herself in Israel with the IDF soldiers.

4,456 Miles

The IDF plane to take Sophie and the FIDF Delegation from the darkness in Poland to Light in Israel.

Sophie and Gita doing the hora on the private IDF plane heading towards Israel with members of the FIDF delegation.

Lori Klisman Ellis

The 911 Living Memorial in Israel with the FIDF delegation. Besides the USA this is the only other place in the world that has the 911 Memorial.

The FIDF Delegation with Benjamin Netanyahu, President of Israel.

Chemi Peres, and Sophie at the FIDF dinner where my mother was honored on 10-29-2019.

(Photos from the FIDF mission were taken by FIDF and Zahava Vidal 2019.)

Conclusion

If you are interested in searching for additional family members, go to Gedmatch genesis and put in Lori's kit number or your kit number and other possible ancestry matches. Then compare the DNA. I hope I inspired you to do your own DNA test if you have not done so yet. It is a thrill to find new family members.

I also hope this book will be a great resource one day for you and your future family members. I am truly blessed to have these people in my life. I only wish I could have met the rest of my loving family. By sharing stories about people who have passed, it will help to keep their memory alive and keep my family tree blooming. Thank you for taking the time to read, learn, and share my family with yours.

I challenge you to do at least one thing to help prevent anti-Semitism. Whether you are a docent, a speaker, share books on anti-Semitism with others, volunteer, donate to the FIDF in honor of my mother, Sophie Tajch Klisman, etc., this will honor all those that perished in the Holocaust as well as honor my family.

Most importantly, remember these messages on behalf of all the Holocaust victims and survivors:

- ✡ *Hatred breeds hatred*
- ✡ *Accept diversity*
- ✡ *We are more alike than different*
- ✡ *Avoid prejudice*
- ✡ *Remember NEVER AGAIN*

Follow this link https://drive.google.com/file/d/0B37-tWdtBdr3aTEzVzdabDBCeTA/view if you would like to view Sophie Tajch Klisman's speech at the Holocaust Memorial Center.

Bibliography

Ancestry, https://www.ancestry.com/.

Bolkosky, Dr. Sidney. "Felicia Shloss—February 9, 1983." *Voice/Vision Holocaust Survivor Oral History Archive*, Board of Regents University of Michigan-Dearborn, February 9, 1983, http://holocaust.umd.umich.edu/schloss/.

Butler, Menachem. "Kissinger on Liberating Ahlem Concentration Camp." *Tablet Magazine*, October 29, 2015, https://www.tabletmag.com/scroll/194615/kissinger-on-liberating-ahlem-concentration-camp.

"CRARG." *Czestochowa-Radomsko Area Research Group*, https://www.crarg.org/.

Desbois, Father Patrick. *In Broad Daylight: The Secret Procedures behind the Holocaust*. New York: Arcade Publishing, 2018.

Draper, Theodore. *The 84th Infantry Division in the Battle of Germany: November 1944-May 1945*. Independently published (pages 244-246), 2018.

Eger, Edith E. *The Choice: Embrace the Possible*. New York: Scribner, 2017.

Frankl, Viktor E. *Man's Search for Meaning*. Boston: Beacon Press, 1992.

"GEDmatch Genesis." *GEDmatch*, https://www.gedmatch.com/.

"Getting Started with GEDmatch—A Segment of DNA." *YouTube*, Family History Fanatics, https://www.youtube.com/watch?v=id7JJ1NoTNk&feature=youtu.be.

Giladi, Ben. "Hedim/Voice," *Bulletins of the American Piotrków Survivors*, Piotrkow-Trybunalski Associations in New York and Israel, http://www.piotrkow-jc.com/en/voice.html.

Harvey, Douglas J. Personal interview, May, 2019.

"Holocaust Trains." *Wikipedia*, en.wikipedia.org/wiki/holocaust_ trains.

Jacobs, A. J. *It's All Relative: Adventures Up and Down the World's Family Tree.* New York: Simon & Schuster, 2017.

Jewish Family Service of Metropolitan Detroit, https://www.jfsdetroit.org/.

JewishGen, an affiliate of the Museum of Jewish Heritage, https://www.jewishgen.org/new/.

Konvisser, Zieva. "Klisman (Teich), Sophie." *Holocaust Memorial Center*, June 24, 2013, https://www.holocaustcenter.org/visit/library-archive/oral-history-department/klisman-teich-sophie/.

Krupa, Gregg. "Holocaust survivor meets ex-GI: 'You gave me my life'." *The Detroit News*, May 13, 2019, updated May 14, 2019, https://www.detroitnews.com/story/news/local/oakland-county/2019/05/13/holocaust-survivor-meets-ex-gi-you-gave-me-my-life/1128611001/.

Kushner, Harold S. *When Bad Things Happen to Good People.* New York: Random House, 1981.

Long, Deborah (Compiler/Translator). "Salzwedel" (unpublished articles from several survivors of Salzwedel Camp, 1988-2006).

Mendelsohn, Jennifer. "No, You Don't Really Have 7,900 4th Cousins: Some DNA Basics for Those with Jewish Heritage." *Medium*, May 23, 2017, https://medium.com/@CleverTitleTK/no-you-dont-really-have-7-900-4th-cousins-some-dna-basics-for-those-with-jewish-heritage-857f873399ff.

Must, Monni, and Sabrina Must. *Living Witnesses—Faces of the Holocaust.* Sylvan Lake, MI: Naturally Photography, 2009.

Silow, Charles. "Bernard Klisman." *Portraits of Honor*, http://portraitsofhonor.org/POHSurvPage.aspx?svid=171.

Silow, Charles. "Sophie Klisman." *Portraits of Honor*, http://portraitsofhonor.org/POHSurvPage.aspx?svid=172.

Spohn, James F. "Reflections of the European Theater." (Unpublished article)

Sucher, Aviva Roth. "2G Second Generation Children Of Holocaust Survivors". *Facebook,* https://www.facebook.com/groups/2GSecongGeneration/.

United States Holocaust Memorial Museum, https://www.ushmm.org/.

Yad Vashem: The World Holocaust Remembrance Center, https://www.yadvashem.org.

"Never forget the 6,000,000 beautiful men, women, and children who perished due to hatred and prejudice."

"Be the one to make a positive impact in this world."

—Sophie Tajch Klisman & Lori Klisman Ellis

Made in the USA
Monee, IL
30 January 2020